Stories of Success:

Only An Irish Boy
(Illustrated)

Stories of Success:

Only An Irish Boy
(Illustrated)

Horatio Alger, Jr.

Sumner Books
Hermosa Beach, CA

Stories of Success:
Only An Irish Boy (Illustrated)
Copyright © 2015 Sumner Books

FIRST EDITION
Sumner Books
737 3rd St
Hermosa Beach, California 90254
310-337-7003
ISBN 978-1-939104-18-2
CREATORS PUBLISHING

Table of Contents

A Note from the Publisher   1
Chapter I: Andy Burke   3
Chapter II: A Skirmish   7
Chapter III: Andy and His Mother   11
Chapter IV: Mrs. Preston   16
Chapter V: A Profitable Job   20
Chapter VI: The Two Old Maids   25
Chapter VII: Andy Gets a Job   30
Chapter VIII: The Midnight Alarm   35
Chapter IX: What Followed   39
Chapter X: Andy's Debut at School   44
Chapter XI: A Game of Ball   49
Chapter XII: A Little Difficulty   54
Chapter XIII: Godfrey's Rebellion   59
Chapter XIV: Mr. Stone Is Called to Account   64
Chapter XV: Mrs. Preston's Discomfiture   69
Chapter XVI: The Christmas Present   73
Chapter XVII: Introduces a Conman   78
Chapter XVIII: Riding With a Highwayman   83
Chapter XIX: Baffled a Robber   88
Chapter XX: How the News Was Received   92
Chapter XXI: A Model Wife   97
Chapter XXII: Colonel Preston's Recovery   102
Chapter XXIII: Mrs. Burke Has Good Fortune   106
Chapter XXIV: Andy's Journey   111
Chapter XXV: The Merchant From Portland   116
Chapter XXVI: Spinning the Web   121
Chapter XXVII: The Drop Game   123
Chapter XXVIII: The Guest of Two Hotels   125
Chapter XXIX: A Startling Event   131
Chapter XXX: Colonel Preston's Will   134
Chapter XXXI: Mrs. Preston's Intentions   138
Chapter XXXII: Mrs. Preston's Revenge   142
Chapter XXXIII: Andy Loses His Job   147
Chapter XXXIV: The Will at Last   151
Chapter XXXV: Mrs. Preston Is Unpleasantly Surprised   155
Chapter XXXVI: All's Well that Ends Well   160
Commentary For Only An Irish Boy by Rick Newcombe   164

Teachers Guide Questions for Only An Irish Boy   167
Teachers Guide Answers for Only An Irish Boy   168
The Life and Themes of Horatio Alger, Jr., by Stefan Kanfer   170
About Horatio Alger, Jr.   175
Our Commitment to Horatio Alger by Rick Newcombe   178
Next in the Stories of Success Series   185

A NOTE FROM THE PUBLISHER

Once crowned "America's most influential writer," Horatio Alger is hardly known today. Those who are familiar with him think "rags to riches," and that's about it. Most young people have never heard of him.

What an opportunity!

More than a hundred years before our contemporary self-help movement, Horatio Alger paved the way with his vivid illustrations of the keys to success and happiness. Today, Sumner Books is excited to introduce a new generation of Americans to some of the most inspirational stories ever written. Regardless of your age, you simply cannot read a Horatio Alger book without coming away with a good feeling.

Alger's books initially sold in the millions and then the tens of millions and finally the hundreds of millions. In fact, the Chicago Daily News once called Horatio Alger "America's best selling author of all time." Sumner Books is committed to bringing to life this best selling collection in the form of audiobooks read by professional actors and recorded with audio engineers in our studio. Our revised e-books, each with a detailed table of contents and colored illustrations, are professionally edited, including the occasional updating of phrases to make the books as easy to read today as they were when they were first published between 1865 and 1900.

Long after his death in 1899, the magazine Publishers Weekly wrote: "To call Horatio Alger Jr. America's most influential writer may seem like an overstatement ... but ... only Benjamin Franklin meant as much to the formation of the American popular mind."

Our goal is to bring back some of the influence that Alger exerted on millions of young people in America. Yes, it's retro; it's counterintuitive and totally contrary to the cynicism that has become a part of American culture. But we are proud to be leading a movement that is as positive and uplifting as the last pages of a Horatio Alger story.

Rick Newcombe
President
Sumner Books

Stories of Success

"If you think you can, you can. And if you think you can't, you're right."
Henry Ford

CHAPTER I

ANDY BURKE

"John, saddle my horse and bring him around to the door."

The speaker was a boy of fifteen, handsomely dressed and, to judge from his air and tone, a person of considerable consequence -- in his own opinion at least. The person addressed was employed in the stable of his father, Colonel Anthony Preston, and so inferior in social condition that Master Godfrey always addressed him in imperious tones.

John looked up and answered respectfully, "Master Godfrey, your horse is sick of a disease, and your father left orders that he wasn't to go out on no account."

"It's my horse," said Godfrey. "I intend to take him out."

"Maybe it's yours, but your father paid for him."

"None of your impudence, John," answered Godfrey angrily. "Am I master, or are you, I should like to know?!"

"Neither, I'm thinking," said John with a twinkle in his eye. "It's your father who's the master."

"I'm master of the horse, anyway, so saddle him at once."

"The colonel would blame me," objected John.

"If you don't, I'll report you and get you dismissed."

"I'll take the risk, Master Godfrey," said the servant good-humoredly. "The colonel won't be so unreasonable as to send me away for obeying his own orders."

Here John was right, and Godfrey knew it, and this vexed him the more. He had an inordinate opinion of himself and his own consequence and felt humiliated at being disobeyed by a servant without being able to punish him for his audacity. This feeling was increased by the presence of a third party who was standing just outside the fence.

As this third party is our hero, I must take a separate paragraph to describe him. He was about the age of Godfrey, possibly a little shorter and stouter. He had a freckled face full of good humor but at the same time was resolute and determined. He appeared to be one who had a will of his own, but not inclined to interfere with others, though ready to stand up for his own rights. In dress he compared very unfavorably with the young aristocrat, who was biting his lips with vexation. In fact, though he is my hero, his dress was far from heroic. He had no vest, and his coat was ragged, as well as his pants. He had on a pair of shoes that were nearly double his size and fit him too largely. He wore a straw hat, for it was summer, but the brim was semi-detached and a part of his brown hair found its way through it.

Now Godfrey was just in the mood for picking a quarrel with somebody, and as there was no excuse for quarreling any further with John, he was rather glad to pitch into the young stranger.

"Who are you?" he demanded in his usual imperious tone and with a contraction of the brow.

"Only an Irish boy!" answered the other with a droll look and an Irish brogue.

"Then what business have you leaning against my fence?" again demanded Godfrey imperiously.

"Shure, I didn't know it was your fence."

"Then you know now. Quit leaning against it."

"Why should I, now? I don't hurt it, do I?"

"No matter -- I told you to go away. We don't want any beggars here."

"Shure, I don't see any," said the other boy demurely.

"What are you but a beggar?"

"Shure, I'm a gentleman of independent fortune."

"You look like it," said Godfrey disdainfully. "Where do you keep it?"

"Here!" said the Irish boy, tapping a bundle wrapped in a red cotton handkerchief, which he carried over his shoulder with a stick thrust through beneath the knot.

"What's your name?"

"Andy Burke. What's yours?"

"I don't feel under any obligation to answer your questions," said Godfrey haughtily.

"Don't you? Then what made you ask me?"

"That's different. You are only an Irish boy."

"And who are you?"

"I am the only son of Colonel Anthony Preston," returned Godfrey impressively.

"Are you, now? I thought you was a royal duke or maybe Queen Victoria's oldest boy."

"Fellow, you are becoming impertinent."

—

4

"Well, I didn't mean it. You look so proud and gintale that it's jist a mistake I made."

"You knew that we had no dukes in America," said Godfrey suspiciously.

"If we had, now, you'd be one of them," said Andy.

"Why? What makes you say so?"

"You're jist the picture of the Earl of Barleycorn's ildest son that I saw before I left Ireland."

Godfrey possessed so large a share of ridiculous pride that he felt pleased with the compliment, though he was not clear about its sincerity.

"Where do you live?" he asked with a slight lowering of his tone.

"Where do I live? Shure, I don't live anywhere now, but I'm going to live in the village. My mother came here a month ago."

"Why didn't you come with her?"

"I was workin' with a farmer, but the work gave out and I came home. Maybe I'll find work here."

"I think I know where your mother lives," said John, who had heard the conversation. "She lives up the road a mile or so, in a little house with two rooms. It's where old Jake Barlow used to live."

"Thank you, sir. I guess I'll be goin' then, as my mother'll be expectin' me. Do you know if she's well?" and a look of anxiety came over the boy's honest, good-natured face.

The question was addressed to John but of this Godfrey was not quite sure. He thought the inquiry was made of him, and his pride was touched.

"What should I know of your mother, you beggar?" he said with a sneer. "I don't associate with such low people."

"Do you mane my mother?" said Andy quickly, and he, too, looked angry and threatening.

"Yes, I do. What are you going to do about it?" demanded Godfrey.

"You'd better take it back," said Andy, his good-humored face now dark with passion.

"Do you think I am afraid of such a beggar as you?" sneered Godfrey. "You appear to forget that you are speaking to a gentleman."

"Shure, I didn't know it," returned Andy hotly. "You're no gentleman if you insult my mother, and if you'll come out here for a minute I'll give you a bating."

"John," said Godfrey angrily, "will you drive that beggar away?"

Now, John's sympathies were rather with Andy than with his young master. He had no great admiration for Godfrey because, during the year he had been in his father's employ, John witnessed too much of the boy's arrogance and selfishness to feel much attachment for him. Had he taken any part in the present quarrel, he would have preferred espousing the cause of the Irish boy, but this would not have been polite, and he therefore determined to preserve his neutrality.

"That ain't my business, Master Godfrey," he said. "You must fight your own battles."

"Go away from here," said Godfrey imperiously advancing toward the part of the fence against which Andy Burke was leaning.

"Will you take back what you said agin' my mother?"

"No, I won't."

"Then you're a blaggard, even if you are a rich man's son."

The blood rushed to Godfrey's face in an instant. This was a palpable insult. What! -- he, a rich man's son, the only son and heir of Colonel Anthony Preston, with his broad acres and an ample bank account -- he to be called a blackguard by a low Irish boy. His passion got the better of him, and he ran through the gate, his eyes flashing fire, bent on exterminating his impudent adversary.

CHAPTER II

A SKIRMISH

Andy Burke was not the boy to run away from an opponent of his own size and age. Neither did he propose to submit quietly to the thrashing which Godfrey designed to give him. He dropped his stick and bundle and squared off scientifically at his aristocratic foe.

Godfrey paused an instant before him.

"I'm going to give you a thrashing," he said. "The worst thrashing you ever had."

"Are you, now?" asked Andy undismayed. "Come on, thin. I'm ready for you."

"You're an impudent young ruffian."

"So are you."

Godfrey's aristocratic blood boiled at this retort, and he struck out at Andy. But the latter knew what was coming and, swift as a flash, warded it off and fetched Godfrey a blow full upon his nose, which then started the blood. Now, the pain combined with the sight of the blood filled him with added fury, and he attempted to seize Andy around the waist and throw him. But here again he was foiled. The young Irish boy evaded his grasp and, seizing him in turn by an adroit movement of the foot, tripped him up. Godfrey fell heavily on his back.

Andy withdrew a little and did not offer to hold him down, as Godfrey would have been sure to do under similar circumstances. "Have you got enough?" he asked.

"That wasn't fair," exclaimed Godfrey jumping up hastily, deeply mortified because he had been humbled in the presence of John, who, sooth to say, rather enjoyed his young master's overthrow.

He rushed impetuously at Andy, but he was blinded by his own impulsiveness, and his adversary, who kept cool and self-possessed, had, of course, the advantage. So the engagement terminated as before -- Godfrey was stretched once more on the sidewalk. He was about to renew the assault, however, when there was an interruption. This interruption came in the form of Colonel Preston himself, who was returning from a business meeting of citizens interested in establishing a savings bank in the village.

"What's all this, Godfrey?" he called out in a commanding tone.

Godfrey knew that when his father spoke he must obey, and he therefore desisted from the contemplated attack. He looked up at his father and said sulkily, "I was punishing this Irish boy for his impertinence."

John grinned a little at this way of putting it, and his father said, "It looked very much as if he were punishing you."

"I didn't get fair hold," said Godfrey sulkily.

"So he was impertinent, was he? What did he say?"

"He said I was no gentleman."

Andy Burke listened attentively to what was said but didn't attempt to justify himself as yet.

"I have sometimes had suspicions of that myself," said his father quietly.

Though Godfrey was an only son, his father was sensible enough to be fully aware of his faults. If he was indulged, it was his mother, not his father, who was at fault. Colonel Preston was a fair and just man and had sensible views about home discipline, but he was overruled by his wife, whose character may be judged from the fact that her son closely resembled her. She was vain, haughty, and proud of putting on airs. She considered herself quite the finest lady in the village but condescended to associate with the wives of the minister, the doctor, and a few of the richer inhabitants. Even with them, however, she took care to show that she regarded herself superior to them all. She was, therefore, unpopular, as was her son among his companions. However, these two stood by each other, and Mrs. Preston was sure to defend Godfrey in all he did and whenever he complained because his father did not do the same.

"I didn't think you'd turn against me and let a low boy insult me," complained Godfrey.

"Why do you call him low?"

"Because he's only an Irish boy."

"Some of our most distinguished men have been Irish boys or of Irish descent. I don't think you have proved your point."

"He's a beggar."

"I'm not a beggar," exclaimed Andy speaking for the first time. "I never begged a penny in all my life."

"Look at his rags," said Godfrey scornfully.

"You would be in rags, too, if you had to buy your own clothes. I think I should respect you very much more under the circumstances," returned his father.

"The colonel's a-givin' it to him," thought John with a grin. "'Twon't do the young master any harm."

"What is your name?" inquired Colonel Preston turning now to our hero, as his son seemed to have no more to say.

"Andy Burke."

"Do you live here?"

"I've just come to town, sir. My mother lives here."

"Where does she live?"

"I don't know yet, sir. He knows," pointing out John.

"I calculate his mother lives in old Jake Barlow's house," said John.

"Oh, the Widow Burke. Yes, I know. I believe Mrs. Preston employs her sometimes. Well, Andy, if that's your name, how is it that I catch you fighting with my son? That is not very creditable, unless you have good cause."

"He called my mother a low woman," said Andy, "and then he run up and hit me."

"Did you do that, Godfrey?"

"He was putting on too many airs. He talked as if he was my equal."

"He appears to be more than your equal in strength," said his father. "Well, was that all?"

"It was about all."

"Then I think he did perfectly right, and I hope you'll profit by the lesson you have received."

"He is a gentleman," thought Andy. "He ain't hard on a boy because he's poor."

Colonel Preston went into the house, but Godfrey lingered behind a moment. He wanted to have a parting shot at his adversary. He could fight with words, if not with blows.

"Look here!" he said imperiously. "Don't let me see you round here again."

"Why not?"

"I don't want to see you."

"Then you can look the other way," said Andy independently.

"This is my house."

"I thought it was your father's."

"That's the same thing. You'd better stay at home with your mother."

—

"Thank you," said Andy. "You're very kind. May I come along the road sometimes?"

"If you do, walk on the other side."

Andy laughed. He was no longer provoked but amused.

"Then, by the same token, you'd better not come by my mother's house," he said good-humoredly.

"I don't want to come near your miserable shanty," said Godfrey disdainfully.

"You may come, if you keep on the other side of the road," said Andy slyly.

Godfrey was getting disgusted, for in the war of words as well as of blows, his ragged opponent seemed to be getting the better of him. He turned on his heel and entered the house. He was sure of one who would sympathize with him in his dislike and contempt for Andy -- this was, of course, his mother. Besides, he had another idea. He knew that Mrs. Burke had been occasionally employed by his mother to assist in the house. It occurred to him that it would be a fine piece of revenge to induce her to dispense hereafter with the poor woman's services. Bent on accomplishing this credible retaliation, he left his young opponent master of the field.

"I must be goin'," said Andy as he picked up his bundle and suspended it from his stick. "Will I easily find the house where my mother lives?"

The question was, of course, addressed to John, who had just turned to go to the stable.

"You can't miss it," answered John. "It's a mile up the road, stands a little way back. There's a few hills of potatoes in the front yard. How long since you saw your mother?"

"It's been three months."

"Does she know you are coming today?"

"No. I would have wrote to her, but my fingers isn't very ready with the pen."

"Nor mine either," said John. "I'd rather take a licking any time than write a letter. Come round and see us sometime."

"The boy'll lick me," said Andy laughing.

"I guess you can manage him."

Andy smiled, for it was also his own conviction. With his bundle on his shoulder he trudged on, light of heart, for he was about to see his mother and sister -- both of whom he warmly loved.

CHAPTER III

ANDY AND HIS MOTHER

The house in which the Widow Burke and her daughter lived was a very humble one. It had not been painted for many years, and the original coat had worn off leaving it dark and time-stained. But when Mrs. Burke came to town a short time before, it was the only dwelling she could obtain that was offered at a rent within her means. So she and Mary, who was now eleven years old, had moved in their scanty furniture and made it look as much like a home as possible.

Mrs. Burke had not always been as poor as she was now. She was the daughter of an Irish tradesman, and she had received quite a good education. In due time she married a small farmer who was considered to be in fair circumstances, but there came a bad year and misfortunes of various kinds came together. The last and heaviest of all was fever, which prostrated her husband on a bed of sickness. Though his wife watched over him night and day with all the devotion of love, it was all of no avail. He died, and she found herself left with about a hundred pounds after his debts were paid. She was advised to go to America with her two children, and she did so. That was five years ago. They had lived in various places and the little sum she had left over, after the passage of the three was paid, had long since melted away, and she was forced to make a living as best she could.

The Widow Burke's humble home in Crampton

Since she had come to Crampton, leaving Andy at work for a farmer in the place where they had last lived, she had obtained what sewing she could from the families in the village as well as an opportunity to help with the ironing at Colonel Preston's. Washing was too hard for her, for her strength was not great.

At the time of our introduction she was engaged in making a shirt, one of half a dozen which she had agreed to make for Dr. Fleming, the village doctor. She had no idea that Andy was so near -- having heard nothing of his having left his job -- but it was of him she was speaking.

"I wish I could see Andy," she sighed looking up from her work.

So do I, mother."

"The sight of him would do my eyes good; he's such a lively lad, Andy is -- always in good spirits."

"Shure, he's got a good heart, mother dear. It wouldn't be so lonely if he were here."

"I would send for him if there were anything for him to do, Mary, but we are so poor that we must all stay where we can get work."

"When do you go to Colonel Preston's, mother? Is it tomorrow?"

"Yes, my dear."

"I'm always lonely when you are away."

"Perhaps you could come with me, Mary, dear. Mrs. Preston wouldn't object, I'm thinkin'."

"If Andy were at home I wouldn't feel so lonely."

While she was speaking Andy himself had crept under the window and heard her words. He was planning a surprise but waited for the last moment to announce himself. He waited to hear what reply his mother would give.

"I think we'll see him soon, Mary, dear."

"What makes you say so, mother?"

"I don't know. I've got a feeling in my bones that we'll soon meet. The blessed saints grant that it may be so."

"Your bones are right this time, mother," said a merry voice.

And Andy, popping up from his stooping position, showed himself at the window.

There was a simultaneous scream from Mary and her mother.

"Is it you, Andy?" exclaimed Mary.

"It isn't nobody else," said Andy rather ungrammatically.

"Come in, Andy, my darling. Come in, and tell me if you are well," said his mother, dropping the shirt on which she was at work and rising to her feet.

"I'll be with you in a jiffy," said Andy.

And, with a light leap, he cleared the window sill and stood in the presence of his mother and sister, who vied with each other in hugging the returned prodigal.

"You'll choke me, Sister Mary," said Andy good-humoredly. "Maybe you think I'm your beau."

"Don't speak to her of beaux; she's only eleven years old," said his mother. "But you haven't told us why you came."

"Well, mother, it was because the work gave out, and I thought I'd pack my trunk and come and see you and Mary. That's all."

"We are glad to see you, Andy, dear, but," continued his mother taking a survey of her son's appearance for the first time, "you're lookin' like a beggar with your clothes all in rags."

Andy laughed.

"Well, it's about so, mother. There was no one to mend 'em for me, and I'm more used to the hoe than the needle."

"I will sew up some of the holes when you've gone to bed, Andy. Are you sure you're well, lad?"

"Well, mother? Jist wait till you see me atin', mother. You'll think I've got a healthy appetite."

"I never doubted it, Andy. The poor lad must be hungry. Mary, see what there is in the closet."

"There's nothing but some bread, mother," said Mary.

Indeed bread and potatoes were the main meals for the mother and daughter, adopted because they were cheap. They seldom ventured on the extravagance of meat, and that was one reason, doubtless, for Mrs. Burke's want of strength and occasional feelings of faintness and dizziness while working at her needle.

"Is there no meat in the house, Mary?"

"Not a bit, mother."

"Then go and see if there's an egg outside."

The widow kept a few hens in a henhouse in one corner of the back yard. The eggs she usually sold, but now that Andy was home and needed something hearty, they had to be more extravagant than usual.

Mary went out and quickly returned with a couple of eggs.

"Here they are, mother, two of them. The black hen was settin' on them, but I drove her away, and you can hear her cackling. Shure, Andy needs them more than she does."

"Will you have them boiled or fried, Andy?" asked his mother.

"Anyway, mother. I'm hungry enough to ate 'em raw. It's hungry work walkin' ten miles wid a bundle on your back, let alone the fightin'."

"Fighting!" exclaimed Mrs. Burke pausing while drawing out the table.

"Fightin', Andy?" chimed in Mary in chorus.

"Yes, mother," said Andy.

"And who did you fight with?" asked the widow anxiously.

"With a boy who feels like he is as big as a king -- maybe bigger."

"What's his name?"

"I heard his father call him Godfrey."

"What, Godfrey Preston?" exclaimed Mrs. Burke in something like consternation.

"Yes, that's the name. He lives in a big house a mile up the road."

"What made you fight with him, Andy?" inquired his mother anxiously.

"He started it."

"What could he have against you? He didn't know you."

"He thought that, as I was only an Irish boy, he could insult me and call me names, but I was too much for him."

"I hope you didn't hurt him?"

"I throwed him twice, mother, but then his father came up and that put a stop to the fight."

"And what did his father say?"

"He took my part, mother, when he found out how it was, and he scolded his son. Shure, he's a gentleman."

"Yes, Colonel Preston is a gentleman."

"And that's where he isn't like his son, I'm thinkin'."

"No. Godfrey isn't like his father. It's his mother he favors."

"Well, I don't call it favoring," said Andy. "Is the old lady as ugly and big-feelin' as the son?"

"She's rather a hard woman, Andy. I go up to work there one day every week."

14

"Do you, mother?" said Andy, not wholly pleased to hear that his mother was employed by the mother of his young enemy.

"Yes, Andy."

"What is it you do?"

"I help about the ironing. Tomorrow's my day for going there."

"I wish you could stay at home and not go out to work, mother," said Andy soberly. "You don't look strong, mother, dear. I'm afraid you're not well."

"Oh, yes, Andy, I am quite well. I shall be better, too, now that you are at home. I missed you very much. It seemed lonely without you."

"I must find some way to earn money, mother," said Andy. "I'm young and strong, and I ought to support you."

"You can help me, Andy," said Mrs. Burke cheerfully.

She took up the shirt and resumed her sewing.

"I'm afraid you're too steady at the work, mother," said Andy.

"I shall be ironing tomorrow. It's a change from sewing, Andy. Mary, it's time to take off the eggs."

Andy was soon eating the frugal meal set before him. He enjoyed it, simple as it was, and left not a particle of the egg or a crumb of the bread.

CHAPTER IV

MRS. PRESTON

Whenever Godfrey Preston had any difficulty with his father, he always went to his mother, and from her -- right or wrong -- he was sure to obtain sympathy. So in the present instance, failing to receive from his father that moral support to which he deemed himself entitled, he entered the house and sought out his mother.

Mrs. Preston, who was rather a spare lady with thin lips and a sharp, hatchet-like face, was in her own room. She looked up as Godfrey entered.

"Well, Godfrey, what's the matter?" she asked, seeing on her son's face an unmistakable expression of discontent.

"Matter enough, mother. Father's always against me."

"I know it. He appears to forget that you are his son. What is it now?"

"He came up just as I was thrashing a boy down in the yard."

"What boy?"

"Nobody you know, mother. It was only an Irish boy."

"What was your reason for punishing him?" asked Mrs. Preston, adopting Godfrey's version of the affair.

"He was impudent to me. He was leaning against the fence, and I ordered him away. He was a ragged boy with a bundle on a stick. Of course, when he wouldn't move, I went out and thrashed him."

"Was your father there?"

"He came up in the midst of it, and, instead of taking my part, he took the part of the Irish boy."

"I don't see how Mr. Preston can be so unfair," said his wife. "It is his duty to stand by his family."

"I felt ashamed to have him scold me before the impudent boy. Of course, he enjoyed it, and I suppose he will think he can be impudent to me again."

"No doubt. I will speak to your father about it. He really shouldn't be so inconsiderate. But what is that stain on your coat, Godfrey? I should think you had been down on your back on the ground."

"Oh," said Godfrey rather embarrassed, "I happened to slip as I was wrestling with the fellow and fell on my back. However, I was up again directly and gave it to him, I can tell you. If father hadn't stopped me I'd have laid him out," he continued in a swaggering tone.

It will be seen that Godfrey did not always confine himself to the truth. Indeed, he found it rather hard at all times to admit either that he had been in the wrong or had been overpowered. Even if his mother sometimes suspected that his accounts were a trifle distorted, she forbore to question their accuracy. Mother and son had a sort of tacit compact by which they stood by each other and made common cause against Colonel Preston.

"Don't you know the boy? Doesn't he live in the neighborhood?" asked Mrs. Preston after a pause.

"He's just come into the town, but I'll tell you who he is. He's the son of that woman that comes to work for you once a week."

"Mrs. Burke?"

"Yes. He told me that his name was Andy Burke."

"He ought to know his place well enough not to be impudent to someone in your position."

"So I think."

"I shall speak to Mrs. Burke about her son's bad behavior."

"I wish you'd discharge her. That's a good way to punish the boy."

"I should object to doing that, Godfrey, because Mrs. Burke is excellent at ironing shirts. Yours and your father's never looked so nice as they have since she has been here."

Godfrey looked a little discontented. Being essentially mean, he thought it would be a remarkable plan to strike the son by way of the mother.

"You might threaten her, mother, a little. Tell her to make her boy behave himself, or you'll discharge her."

"I will certainly speak to her on the subject, Godfrey."

At the table Mrs. Preston introduced the subject of Godfrey's injuries.

"I am surprised, Mr. Preston, that you took part against Godfrey when he was rudely assaulted this morning."

"I thought Godfrey in the wrong, my dear. That was my reason."

"You generally appear to think your own son in the wrong. You are ready to take part with any stranger against him," said Mrs. Preston in a complaining manner.

"I don't think you are quite right just there," said her husband good-humoredly. "I must say, however, that Godfrey generally is in the wrong."

"You are very unjust to him."

"I don't mean to be. I would be glad to praise him, but he is so overbearing to those whom he considers his inferiors that I am frequently ashamed of his manner of treating others."

"The boy has some reason to feel proud. He must maintain his position."

"What is his position?"

"I don't think you need to ask. As our son he is entitled to a degree of consideration."

"He will receive consideration enough if he deserves it, but this is a republic, and all are supposed to be equal."

Mrs. Preston tossed her head.

"That's well enough to say, but don't you consider yourself above a man that goes round sawing wood for a living?"

"At any rate I would treat him with courtesy. Because I am richer and have a better education is no reason why I should treat him with contempt."

"Then I don't share your sentiments," said Mrs. Preston. "I am thankful that I know my position better. I mean to uphold the dignity of the family, and I hope my son will do the same."

Colonel Preston shrugged his shoulders as his wife swept from the room. He long knew her sentiments on this subject, and he was aware that she was not likely to become a convert to his more democratic ideas.

"I am afraid she will spoil Godfrey," he thought. "The boy is getting intolerable. I am glad this Irish boy gave him a lesson. He seems a fine-spirited lad. I will help him if I can."

"Ellen," said Mrs. Preston the next morning, "when Mrs. Burke comes let me know."

"Yes, ma'am."

"She's come," announced Ellen half an hour later.

Mrs. Preston rose from her seat and went into the laundry.

"Good morning, Mrs. Preston," said Mrs. Burke.

"Good morning," returned the other stiffly. "Mrs. Burke, I hear that your son behaved very badly to my Godfrey yesterday."

"It isn't like Andy, ma'am," said the mother quietly. "He's a good, well-behaved lad."

"Godfrey tells me that he made a brutal assault upon him, quite forgetting his superior position."

"Are you sure Master Godfrey didn't strike him first?" asked the mother.

"Even if he had, your son shouldn't have struck back."

"Why not?" asked Mrs. Burke, her eyes flashing with spirit, though meek as she generally was.

"Because it was improper," said Mrs. Preston decisively.

"I don't see that, ma'am. Andy isn't the boy to stand still and be struck."

"Do I understand," said Mrs. Preston in a freezing tone, "that you uphold your son in his atrocious conduct?"

"Yes, ma'am. I stand up for Andy, for he's a good boy, and if he struck Master Godfrey it was because he was struck first."

"That is enough," said Mrs. Preston angrily. "I shall not require your services after today, Mrs. Burke."

"Just as you like, ma'am," said Mrs. Burke with quiet pride but thought, with a sinking heart, of the gap which this would make in her scanty income.

CHAPTER V

A PROFITABLE JOB

After finishing her work at Colonel Preston's, Mrs. Burke went home. She did not see Mrs. Preston again, for the latter sent the money for her services by Ellen.

"Mrs. Preston says you're not to come next week," said Ellen.

"She told me so herself this morning. She is angry because I took the part of my boy against Master Godfrey."

"Godfrey's the hatefulest boy I ever see," said Ellen, whose grammar was a little defective. "He's always putting on airs."

"He struck my Andy, and Andy struck him back."

"I'm glad he did," said Ellen emphatically. "I hope he'll do it again."

"I don't want the boys to fight. Andy's a peaceable lad, and he'll be quiet if he's let alone. But he's just like his poor father, and he won't let anybody trample on him."

"That's where he's right," said Ellen. "I'm sorry you're not coming again, Mrs. Burke."

"So am I, Ellen, for I need the money, but I'll stand by my boy."

"You iron real beautiful. I've heard Mrs. Preston say so often. She won't get nobody that'll suit her so well."

"If you hear of anybody else that wants help, Ellen, will you send them to me?"

This Ellen faithfully promised, and Mrs. Burke went home, sorry to have lost her engagement but not sorry to have stood up for Andy of whom she was proud.

Andy was at home when she returned. He had found enough to do at home to occupy him so far. The next day he meant to go out in search of employment. When his mother got back she found him cutting some brush which he had obtained from the neighboring woods.

"There, mother," he said pointing to a considerable pile. "You'll have enough sticks to last you a good while."

"Thank you, Andy, dear. That'll save Mary and me a good deal of trouble."

There was nothing in her words, but something in her tone which led Andy to ask, "What's the matter, mother? Has anything happened?"

"I've got through working for Mrs. Preston, Andy."

"Got through? For today, you mean?"

"No. I'm not going to work there again."

"Why not?"

"She complained of you, Andy."

"What did she say, mother?" asked our hero listening with attention.

"She said you ought not to have struck Godfrey."

"Did you tell her he struck me first?"

"Yes, I did."

"And what did she say, thin?"

"She said that you ought not to have struck him back."

"And what did you say, mother?"

"I said my Andy wasn't the boy to stand still and let anybody beat him."

"Good for you, mother! Bully for you! That's where you hit the nail on the head. And what did the ould lady say then?"

"She told me I needn't go back there again to work."

"I'm glad you're not goin', mother. I don't want you to work for the likes of her. Let her do her own ironin', the ould spalpeen!"

In general, Andy's speech was tolerably clear of the brogue, but whenever he became a little excited, as at present, it was more marked, which is he why he used the Irish word spalpeen instead of rascal. He was more angry at the slight to his mother than he would have been at anything, however contemptuous, said to himself. He had that chivalrous feeling of respect for his mother which every boy of his age ought to have, more especially if that mother is a widow.

"But, Andy, I'm very sorry for the money I'll lose."

"How much is it, mother?"

"Seventy-five cents."

"I'll make it up, mother."

"I know you will if you can, Andy, but work is hard to get, and the pay is small."

"You might go back and tell Mrs. Preston that I'm a dirty spalpeen, and maybe she'd take you back, mother."

"I wouldn't slander my own boy like that if she'd take me back twenty times."

"That's the way to talk, mother," said Andy well pleased. "Don't you be afeared -- we'll get along somehow. It's only a token, but here's three dollars I brought home with me yesterday."

Andy pulled out of his pocket six silver half-dollars and offered them to his mother.

"Where did you get them, Andy?" she asked in surprise.

"Where did I get them? One way and another by overwork. We won't starve while them last, will we?"

Andy's cheerful tone had its effect upon his mother.

"Perhaps you're right, Andy," she said smiling. "At any rate we won't cry till it's time."

"Tomorrow I'll go out and see if I can find work."

"Suppose you don't find it, Andy?" suggested his sister.

"Then I'll take in washing," said Andy laughing. "It's an iligant washer I'd make, wouldn't I now?"

"Nobody'd hire you more than once, Andy."

By and by they had supper. If they had been alone they would have got along on bread and tea, but, "Andy needs meat, for he's a growing boy," said his mother.

And so Mary was dispatched to the butcher's for a pound and a half of beefsteak, which made the meal considerably more attractive. Mrs. Burke felt that it was extravagant, particularly just as her income was diminished, but she couldn't bear to stint Andy. At first she was not going to eat herself, meaning to save a part for Andy's breakfast, but our hero found her out and declared he wouldn't eat a bit if his mother did not eat, too. So she was forced to take her share, and it did her good, for no one can keep up a decent share of strength on bread and tea alone.

The next morning Andy went out in search of work. He had no very definite idea where to go or to whom to apply, but he concluded to put in an application anywhere he could.

He paused in front of the house of Deacon Jones, a hard-fisted old farmer whose reputation for parsimony was well known throughout the village, but of this Andy, being a newcomer, was ignorant.

"Wouldn't you like to hire a good strong boy?" he asked, entering the yard.

The deacon looked up.

"Ever worked on a farm?"

"Yes."

"Can you milk?"

"Yes."

"Where did you work?"

"In Carver."

"What's your name?"

"Andy Burke."

"Where do you live?"

"With my mother, Mrs. Burke, a little way down the road."

"I know -- the Widder Burke."

"Have you got any work for me?"

"Wait a minute, I'll see."

The deacon brought out an old scythe from the barn and felt the edge. There was not much danger in so doing, for it was as dull as a hoe.

"This scythe needs sharpening," he said. "Come and turn the grindstone."

"Well, here's a job, anyhow," thought Andy. "Wonder what he'll give me."

He sat down and began to turn the grindstone. The deacon bore on heavily, and this made it hard turning. His arms ached, and the perspiration stood on his brow. It was certainly pretty hard work, but then he must be prepared for that, and after all he was earning money for his mother. Still the time did seem long. The scythe was so intolerably dull that it took a long time to make any impression upon it.

"Kinder hard turnin', ain't it?" said the deacon.

"Yes," said Andy.

"This scythe ain't been sharpened for ever so long. It's as dull as a hoe."

However, time and patience work wonders, and at length the deacon, after a careful inspection of the blade of the scythe, released Andy from his toil of an hour and a half with the remark, "I reckon that'll do."

He put the scythe in its place and came out.

Andy lingered respectfully for the remuneration of his labor.

"He ought to give me a quarter," he thought. But the deacon showed no disposition to pay him, and Andy became impatient.

"I guess I'll be goin'," he said.

"All right. I ain't got anything more for you to do," said the deacon.

"I'll take my pay now," said Andy desperately.

"Pay? What for?" inquired the deacon innocently.

"For turning the grindstone."

"You don't mean ter say you expect anything for that?" said the deacon in a tone of surprise.

"Yes I do," said Andy. "I can't work an hour and a half for nothing."

"I didn't expect to pay for such a trifle," said the old man fumbling in his pocket.

Finally he brought out two cents, one of the kind popularly known as bung-towns, which are not generally recognized as true currency.

"There," he said in an injured tone. "I'll pay you, though I didn't think you'd charge anything for any little help like that."

Andy looked at the proffered compensation with mingled astonishment and disgust.

"Never mind," he said. "You can keep it. You need it more'n I do, I'm thinkin'!"

"Don't you want it?" asked the deacon surprised.

"No, I don't. I'm a poor boy, but I don't work an hour and a half for two cents, one of 'em bad. I'd rather take no pay at all."

"That's a cur'us boy," said the deacon slowly sliding the pennies back into his pocket. "I calc'late he expected more just for a little job like that. Does he think I'm made of money?"

As Andy went out of the yard, the idea dawned upon the deacon that he had saved two cents, and his face was luminous with satisfaction.

CHAPTER VI

THE TWO OLD MAIDS

"He's the meanest man I ever saw," thought Andy. "Does he think I work on nothing a year, and find myself? Divil a bit of work will I do for him agin, if I know it." But better luck was in store for Andy. Quarter of a mile farther on, in a two-story, old-fashioned but neat house, lived two maiden ladies of very uncertain age -- Misses Priscilla and Sophia Grant. I am not aware that any relationship existed between them and our distinguished ex-President. Nevertheless, they were of very respectable family and connections and of independent property -- each owned bank stock which brought them in an annual income of about twelve hundred dollars, in addition to the house they occupied and half a dozen acres of land thereunto pertaining. Now, this was not a colossal fortune, but in a country place like Crampton it made them ladies of large property.

The Misses Grant home in the village of Campton

Priscilla was the elder of the two and the general manager. Sophia contented herself with being the echo of her stronger-minded sister and was very apt to assent to her remarks, either by repeating them or by saying, "Just so." She was a mild, inoffensive creature but very charitable and amiable, and she was so little given to opposition that there was always the greatest harmony between them. They kept a gardener, or outdoor servant, for all types of work, who cultivated the land, sawed and split their wood, ran errands, and made himself generally useful. He had one drawback, unfortunately. He would occasionally indulge in excess in certain fiery alcoholic compounds sold at the village tavern and, as natural consequence, got drunk. He had usually the good sense to keep out of the way while under the influence of liquor, and until now the good ladies had borne with him and retained him in their employ.

But a crisis had arrived. That morning he had come for orders while inebriated, and in his drunken folly had actually gone so far as to call Miss Priscilla "darling" and offer to kiss her.

Miss Priscilla was, of course, horrified, and so expressed herself.

"Law, Sophia," she said, "I came near fainting away. The idea of his offering to kiss me."

"Just so," said Sophia.

"So presuming."

"Just so."

"Of course, I couldn't think of employing him any longer."

"Couldn't think of it."

"He might have asked to kiss me again."

"Just so."

"Or you!"

"Just so," said Sophia in some excitement of manner.

"The neighbors would talk."

"Indeed."

"So I told him that I was very sorry, but it would be necessary for him to find work somewhere else."

"But who will do our work?" inquired Sophia with a rare, original suggestion.

"We must get somebody else."

"So we must," acquiesced Sophia as if she had suddenly received light on a very dark subject.

"But I don't know who we can get."

"Just so."

At that moment there was a knock at the door. Priscilla answered it herself. They kept no domestic servant, only a gardener.

"I've brought the load of wood you ordered, ma'am," said a delivery man. "Where shall I put it?"

"In the backyard. John -- no, John has left us. I will show you myself."

She put on a cape-bonnet and indicated the place in the yard where she wanted the wood dumped.

Then she returned to the house.

"It's very awkward that John should have acted so," she said in a tone of annoyance. "I don't know who is to saw and split that wood."

"We couldn't do it ourselves," said Sophia with another original suggestion.

"Of course not. That would be perfectly absurd."

"Just so."

"I don't believe there is enough wood sawed and split to last through the day."

"We must have some split."

"Of course. But I really don't know of anyone in the neighborhood that we could get."

"John."

"John has gone away. You know why."

"Perhaps he wouldn't kiss us if we told him not to," suggested Sophia.

"I am afraid you are a goose," said Priscilla composedly.

"Just so," slipped out of Sophia's mouth from force of habit, but her sister was so used to hearing it that she took no particular notice of it on the present occasion.

It was just at this time that Andy, released from his severe and unrequited labor for Deacon Jones, came by. He saw the wood being unloaded in the back yard, and an idea struck him.

"Maybe I can get the chance of sawin' and splittin' that wood. I'll try, anyway. I wonder who lives there?"

He immediately opened the front gate and, marching up to the front door, knocked vigorously.

"There's somebody at the door," said Sophia.

"Perhaps it's John who has come back," said Priscilla. "I am afraid of going to open it. He might want to kiss me again."

"I'll go," said Sophia rising with unwonted alacrity.

"He might want to kiss you."

"I'll tell him not to."

"We'll both go," said Priscilla decisively.

Accordingly the two sisters, for mutual protection, both went to the door and opened it guardedly. Their courage returned when they saw that it was only a boy.

"What do you want?" asked Priscilla.

"Just so," chimed in Sophia.

"You've got a load of wood in the back yard," commenced Andy.

"Just so," said Sophia.

"Do you want it sawed and split?"

The younger sister brightened up.

"Can you do it?" inquired Priscilla.

"Try me and see," answered Andy.

"You're not a man."

"Just so," chimed in her sister.

"Well, I soon will be," said Andy. "I can saw and split wood as well as any man you ever saw."

"What is your name?"

"Andy Burke."

"Are you a -- Hibernian?" inquired Priscilla.

"I don't know what you mane by that name," said Andy perplexed.

"To what nation do you belong?"

"Oh, that's what you want, ma'am. I'm only an Irish boy."

"And you say your name is Burke?"

"Yes, ma'am."

"Are you related to Burke, the great orator? He was an Irishman, I believe."

"Just so," said Sophia.

"He was my great-grandfather, ma'am," answered Andy, who had never heard of the eminent orator, but thought the claim would improve his chances of obtaining the job of sawing and splitting wood.

Edmund Burke was a statesman, author, orator, political theorist and philosopher who lived in the mid 18th century.

"Your great-grandfather!" exclaimed Priscilla in astonishment.

"Really, this is most extraordinary. And you are poor?"

"If I wasn't I wouldn't be goin' round sawin' wood, ma'am."

"To think that the grandson of the great Burke should come to us for employment," said Priscilla, who was in some respects easily taken in. "I think we must hire him, Sophia."

"Just so."

"Perhaps he could take John's place altogether."

"Just so."

"I must find out whether he understands gardening."

"Indeed."

Andy stood by waiting patiently for the decision and hoping that it might be favorable. Of course, it was wrong for him to tell a lie, but he thought his engagement depended upon it, and although a very good boy for the most part, he was not altogether perfect, as my readers are destined to find out.

CHAPTER VII

ANDY GETS A JOB

"Do you understand the care of a garden?" asked Miss Priscilla.

"Yes," answered Andy promptly.

"Then you are used to agricultural labor?"

"I've been workin' on a farm all summer."

"Our man has just left us, and we must hire somebody else."

"Just so," chimed in Sophia.

"And if you are competent -- "

"Try me," said Andy.

"I really think we'd better, Sophia," said Priscilla turning to her sister.

"Just so."

"We'll try you for a week. What compensation do you require?"

"Is it wages you mane? How much did you give the man you had before me?" asked Andy shrewdly.

"Twenty-five dollars a month and board."

"That'll suit me," said Andy audaciously.

At the farmer's for whom he had been working he had received board and a dollar a week.

"But you are a boy. Men folks get more than boys."

"I'll do as much work as he did any day," said Andy stoutly.

"I really don't know what to say. I think we'll give you five dollars the first week, and then we will decide about the future."

"I'm to eat here?" inquired Andy.

"Yes, you will make your home here. We will put you in John's room."

"When shall I begin?"

"We shall need some wood split at once."

"All right, ma'am, but it's lunch time. I'll just go home and get a bite to keep up my strength."

"You can have your lunch here. It will be ready in half an hour."

"Just so."

"All right," said Andy. "I'm agreeable."

"Do you live in the village?"

"I do now. My mother lives up the road a bit."

"Very well. Go and split some wood, and we'll call you in to lunch. You'll find the ax and the saw in the shed."

Andy found the articles referred to and straightaway went to work. He was really a "smart boy to work," as the phrase is, and he went to work with a will. He was greatly elated at having secured so profitable a job. He meant to give satisfaction so as to keep the job. Five dollars a week and board seemed to him a magnificent income, and it compared very favorably with his wages at Farmer Bellnap's where he had been working all summer.

"It's lucky I came here," he said to himself as he plied the saw energetically, "but what queer old ladies they are, especially the one that's always sayin' 'Just so.' If I'd tell her I'd got fifty-seven grandchildren I'll bet she'd say, 'Just so.'"

Miss Sophia was looking out of the back window to see how their new "man" worked. Occasionally Priscilla, as she was setting the table, glanced out of the window in passing.

"He takes hold as if he knew how," she observed.

"Just so," responded her sister.

"I think he works faster than John."

"Just so."

"It's very strange that he should be the great-grandson of the great Burke."

"Indeed."

"And that he should be sawing wood for us, too."

"Quite right."

"I think we must be kind to him, sister."

"Just so. He won't try to kiss you, Priscilla," said Sophia with a sudden thought.

"You are a goose, sister," said Priscilla.

"Just so," assented the other from force of habit.

In due time lunch was ready, and Andy was summoned from the woodpile. He was in no way sorry for the summons. He had a hearty appetite at all times, and just now it was increased by his unrequited labor in turning the grindstone for Deacon Jones as well as by the half-hour he had spent at his new task.

The Misses Grant did their own work, as I have before observed. They were excellent cooks, and the lunch now upon the table, though plain, was very savory and inviting. Andy's eyes fairly danced with satisfaction as they rested on the roast beef and vegetables, which emitted an odor of a highly satisfactory character. At the farmer's where he had last worked the table had been plentifully supplied, but the cooking was very rudimentary.

"Sit down, Andrew," said Miss Priscilla. "I think that is your name."

"They call me 'Andy,' ma'am."

"That means Andrew. Shall I give you some meat?"

"Thank you, ma'am."

"Will you have it rare or well done?"

"Well done, ma'am. I have it rare enough, anyhow. In fact, almost never."

"Sophia, Andrew has made a joke," said Priscilla with a decorous smile.

"Just so, Priscilla," and Sophia smiled also.

"I suppose your family has been reduced to poverty, Andrew, or you would not be seeking employment of this character?"

"True for you, ma'am," said Andy with his mouth full.

"How was your family property lost?"

"Well, ma'am, by speculation," said Andy hazarding a guess.

"That is very sad. Sophia, we must never speculate."

"Just so, Priscilla."

"Or we might lose all our money."

"And have to saw wood for a living," said Sophia with another brilliant idea.

Andy was so amused at the picture thus suggested that he came near choking but recovered himself after a violent attack of coughing.

"I am afraid, Sophia, we should scarcely make a living in that way," said Priscilla with a smile.

"Quite right," acquiesced her sister.

"How long have you been in this country, Andrew?"

"Six years, ma'am."

Andy kept at work industriously. His appetite proved to be quite equal to the supply of food, but his evident enjoyment of the lunch only gratified the ladies, who, though eccentric, were kind-hearted and not in the least mean.

"What will I do, ma'am?" asked our hero.

"You may go on sawing wood."

So Andy resumed work, and he worked faithfully during the afternoon. By this time there was a large pile of wood ready for the stove.

At half-past four Miss Priscilla appeared at the door.

"Andrew," she said.

"Yes, ma'am."

"Do you feel tired?"

"A little, ma'am."

"Does your mother know you are here?"

"No, ma'am."

"Would you like to go home and tell her?"

"Yes, ma'am, I would."

"You can go now or after supper, as you prefer."

"Then I'll go now."

"But remember, we want you to come back and sleep here. We do not feel safe without a man in the house."

Andy felt rather flattered at being referred to as a man.

"I'll be back any time you name, ma'am," he said.

"Then be back here at nine o'clock."

"Very well, ma'am."

Andy put on his coat and hurried home. He wanted to tell his mother and Mary the good news about his engagement at such unexpected good wages.

Mrs. Burke looked up inquiringly as he entered the house.

"Where have you been, Andy?" she asked. "I thought I had lost you."

"You don't lose me so easy, mother. Shure, I've been at work."

"At work?"

"Yes -- I've got a job."

"What, already? You are lucky, Andy."

"You'll think so, mother. How much do you think I get besides board, mind?"

"A dollar a week?"

"What do you say to three dollars?"

"You're a lucky boy, Andy. I'm glad for you."

"What do you say to five dollars a week, mother?" asked Andy in exultation.

"You're jokin' now, Andy," said his sister. "I don't believe you've got a job at all."

"I have, and it's five dollars a week I'm to get. Ask the ould maids I'm workin' for."

"The Miss Grants?"

"I expect so. They're mighty queer old ladies. One of 'm is always sayin', 'Just so.'"

"That is Miss Sophia Grant."

33

"Just so," said Andy mimicking her.

"You mustn't do that, Andy. Then it's them you're workin' for?"

"Yes, and they're mighty kind. I'm goin' back to sleep there tonight. They want a man to purtect them."

Mary laughed.

"Do you call yourself a man, Andy? What could you do if a burglar tried to get in?"

"I'd give him what Paddy gave the drum," said Andy.

"Supper is ready," announced his mother.

It was a cheerful meal. Andy had done much better than his mother expected, and it seemed likely that they would get along in spite of her being discharged by Mrs. Preston.

CHAPTER VIII

THE MIDNIGHT ALARM

"It's time for me to be goin' back," said Andy as the clock indicated twenty minutes to nine.

"I wish you could sleep at home, Andy," said his mother.

"They want me to purtect them," said our hero with a little importance. "I'll pack my clothes in a handkerchief."

"I've got a little carpetbag," said his mother. "That looks more respectable. When you have earned enough money, you must have a new suit of clothes."

"How much will they cost, mother?"

"I think we can get a cheap suit for fifteen or twenty dollars. When you have got the money, we will call on the tailor and see."

"Shure, I'll feel like a gentleman with a suit like that."

"Mary, go and get the carpetbag. I've packed Andy's clothes all ready for him."

Mary soon reappeared with the carpetbag, and Andy set out on his return.

Presently, as the clock struck nine, he knocked at the door of the Misses Grant. The elder opened the door for him.

"You are punctual, Andrew," she said approvingly.

"Yes, ma'am."

"Are those your clothes?" pointing to the bag he carried.

"What few I've got, ma'am. I'm goin' to buy some more when I've got money enough."

"That is right. We want you to look respectable."

"Just so," remarked Sophia, who felt that it was time for her to speak.

Then a brilliant idea seized her.

"If he were a girl, we could give him some of our dresses."

"But he isn't," said matter-of-fact Priscilla.

"Or if we were men," continued Sophia with another brilliant idea.

"But we are not."

"Just so," assented her sister, now brought to the end of her suggestions.

By this time Andy was in the house, holding his cap in one hand and his carpetbag in the other.

"Do you feel tired?" asked Priscilla.

"Yes, ma'am."

"Then, perhaps you would like to go to bed?"

"I would, if it's just the same to you, ma'am."

"Very well. Follow me, and I will show you your room. Sophia, perhaps you had better come too."

They went up the front stairs. The house proper had two rooms on the lower floor and the two chambers over them. But there was also an extension behind, used as a kitchen, and over this was the room which had been used by John, the former servant.

"This is your room, Andrew," said Miss Priscilla. "Sophia, will you lift the latch?"

The door, upon opening, revealed a small chamber with the ceiling partly sloping. There were two windows. It was very plainly furnished but looked very comfortable. Andy glanced about him with a look of satisfaction. It was considerably more attractive than the bed in the attic which he had occupied at the house of the farmer for whom he had last worked.

"We've put the feather bed at the bottom, as it's summer," said Miss Priscilla.

"All right, ma'am."

"There's one thing you've forgotten, Priscilla," suggested Sophia.

"What is that?"

"The gun."

"Oh, yes. I am glad you reminded me of it. Andrew, can you fire off a gun?"

"Yes, ma'am," said Andrew glibly.

He had never done it, but he had seen a gun fired and always wanted to make a trial himself.

"As you are the only menfolks in the house, we should expect you to fire at any robbers that try to enter the house."

"Do you expect any, ma'am?" asked Andy eagerly.

"No, but some might come. Of course, we cannot fire guns -- it would be improper, as we are ladies."

"Quite right," interrupted Sophia.

"So we shall leave that to you. Do you think you would dare to?"

"Would I dare, is it?" asked Andy. "Shure, I'd be glad of the chance."

"I see you are brave. I'll show you the gun now."

She went to the closet in the corner of the room and pointed out a big, unwieldy musket to Andy. It was in the corner.

"Is it loaded, ma'am?" he asked.

"Yes. It has been loaded for a year or more. John never had occasion to use it, and I hope you won't. If any robber should come," added the kind-hearted spinster, "perhaps you had better only shoot him in the arm and not kill him."

"Just as you say, ma'am."

"I believe that is all I have to say. Sophia, shall we go to our own room?"

"Indeed."

So the two maidens withdrew, and Andy was left to his own reflections. He undressed himself quickly and deposited himself in the bed which proved to be very comfortable.

He went to bed, but there was one thing that prevented his going to sleep. This was the gun. He had never even had one in his hand, and now there was one at his absolute disposal. It made him feel a sense of his importance to feel that upon him, young as he was, devolved the duty of defending the house and its occupants from burglary.

"And why not? Shure, I'm 'most a man," reflected Andy. "I can shoot off a gun as well as anybody. I wonder if robbers will come tonight!" thought Andy.

He rather wished they would so that he might have an excuse for firing the gun. However, of this there seemed very little chance, for had not Miss Priscilla said that it had been loaded for more than a year, and during all that time John had never had occasion to use it? This seemed rather discouraging.

"I wonder, would they let me go out shooting with it?" thought Andy.

Somehow or another, he could not get his mind off the gun, and after a lapse of an hour he was as wide awake as ever.

Meanwhile, Priscilla and Sophia were both asleep, not being interested in the gun.

Finally it occurred to Andy that he would get up and look at the gun. He wanted to make sure that he understood how to fire it. It was important that he should do so, he reasoned to himself, for might not a burglar come that very night? Then, suppose he was unable to fire the gun, and in consequence of his ignorance both he and the two ladies should be murdered in their beds. Of course, this was not to be thought of, so Andy got out of bed and, finding a match, lit the candle and put it on the bureau -- or chest of drawers, as they called it in the country.

Then he stepped softly to the closet and took out the gun.

"Murder! How heavy it is!" thought Andy. "I didn't think it was half as heavy. There must be a pound of bullets inside. Now," he said to himself, "suppose a big thafe was to poke his dirty head in at the winder and say, 'Give me all your money, or I'll break your head' -- I'd put up the gun and point at him this way."

Here Andy brought the gun into position with some difficulty and put his finger near the trigger.

"And I'd say," continued Andy rehearsing his part, "'Jump down, you thafe, or I'll put a bullet through your head.'"

At that unlucky moment his finger accidentally pulled the trigger, and instantly there was a tremendous report, the noise increased by the shattering of the window panes by the bullet.

Probably the charge was too heavy, for the gun "kicked," and Andy, to his astonishment, found himself lying flat on his back on the floor with the gun lying beside him.

"Oh, murder!" exclaimed the bewildered boy, "Is it dead I am? Shure, the divil's in the gun. What will the ould wimmen say? They'll think it's bloody burglars gettin' into the house. Shure, I'll slip on my pants, for they'll be coming to see what's happened."

He picked himself up and slipped on his pants. He had scarcely got them on when the trembling voice of Miss Priscilla was heard at the door.

CHAPTER IX

WHAT FOLLOWED

The report of the gun, as may be supposed, had aroused both the ladies from their sleep.

"Did you hear it?" cried Miss Priscilla clutching her sister by the arm.

"Just so," muttered Sophia in bewilderment. "It's the gun." Then she exclaimed in alarm, "Burglars!"

"I am afraid so. What shall we do?"

"Run away," suggested Sophia.

"No, we must not leave the boy to be murdered."

"Perhaps he has shot them?" said Sophia with a gleam of hope.

"At any rate, it is our duty to go and see what has happened."

"I'm afraid," whimpered Sophia covering up her head.

"Then you can stay here," said the more courageous Priscilla. "I will go."

"And leave me alone?"

"I must."

"I'll go too, then," said Sophia, her teeth clattering with fear.

So they crept out of bed and, throwing shawls over their shoulders, advanced into the entry, trembling with excitement and fear.

"What if we should find Andy weltering in his gore?" suggested Priscilla.

"Don't say such horrid things, or I shall scream," said her sister.

Then came the tremulous knock mentioned at the close of the last chapter.

Andy opened the door in person and met the gaze of the two Misses Grant, Sophia almost ready to drop with fright.

"Do you see any gore, Priscilla?" she asked tremulously.

"Are you hurt, Andrew?" asked the elder sister.

"No, ma'am."

"Did you fire the gun?"

"Yes, ma'am."

"What made you? Did any burglars try to get in?"

"Not exactly, ma'am," said Andy, "but I thought there might be some."

"Did you see any?"

"Not exactly," said Andy, a little embarrassed," but I heard a noise."

"Just so," said Sophia.

"Why didn't you wait till they appeared at the window, Andrew?"

"Because, ma'am, they would fire at me first. I wanted to scare 'em away."

"Perhaps you were right. You don't see any traces of them outside, do you?"

"You can look for yourself, ma'am."

The two ladies went to the window, which, as already explained, had suffered from the discharge, and peered out timidly, but of course they saw no burglars.

"Are you sure there were burglars, Andrew?" asked Priscilla.

"No, ma'am, I couldn't swear to it."

"Well, no harm has been done."

"Except breakin' the winder, ma'am."

"Never mind. We will have that mended tomorrow."

"Were you afraid, Andrew?" asked Miss Sophia.

"Not a bit," answered Andy valiantly. "I ain't afraid of burglars, as long as I have a gun. I'm a match for 'em."

"How brave he is!" exclaimed the timid lady. "We might have been killed in our beds. I'm glad we hired him, Priscilla."

"As there is nothing more to do, we had better go to bed."

"Just so."

"That's a bully way to get out of a scrape," said Andy to himself as the ladies filed out of his chamber. "I expected they'd scold me. Plague take the old gun -- it kicks as bad as a mule. Oh, Andy, you're a lucky boy to get off so well."

The next day Andy obtained permission to take out the gun in the afternoon when his chores were done.

"I want to get used to it, ma'am," he said. "It kicked last night."

"Dear me, did it?" asked Sophia. "I didn't know guns kicked. What do they kick with? They haven't got any legs."

Andy explained as well as he could what he meant by the gun's kicking and said it was because it had not been used for a good while and needed to be taken out.

"It needs exercise, just like horses, ma'am," he said.

"That is singular, Andrew," said Priscilla.

"Just so," observed her sister.

"It's a fact, ma'am," said Andy. "It gets skittish just like horses, but if I take it out sometimes, it'll be all right."

"Very well, you may take it -- only be careful."

"Oh, I'll be careful, ma'am," said Andy with alacrity.

"Now, I'll have some fun," he said to himself.

He found a supply of powder and some shot in the closet and proceeded to appropriate them.

"Come back in time for supper, Andrew," said Miss Priscilla.

"Yes, ma'am, I'm always on hand at mealtimes," answered our hero.

"That's because he's hungry," said Sophia brilliantly.

"You're right, ma'am," said Andy. "My stomach always tells me when it's supper time."

"It's as good as a watch," said Priscilla smiling.

"And a good deal cheaper," observed Sophia with another brilliant idea.

Andy started up the road with his gun over his shoulder. It was his intention, after going a little distance, to strike into the fields and make for some woods not far away where he thought there would be a good chance for birds or squirrels. He hadn't gone many steps before he encountered Godfrey Preston, his antagonist of three days previous.

Now, Godfrey hadn't seen or heard anything of Andy since that day. He had learned from his mother with great satisfaction that she had discharged Mrs. Burke from her employment, as this, he imagined, would trouble Andy. But of Andy himself he knew nothing, and he was not aware that he had already secured a job. When he saw our hero coming along, his curiosity led him to stop and find out, if he could, where he was going with the gun he carried on his shoulder and where he had obtained it. So he looked intently at Andy, waiting for him to speak, but Andy preferred to leave that to Godfrey.

"Whose gun is that?" asked Godfrey, in the tone of one who was entitled to ask the question.

"Shure, it belongs to the owner," said Andy with a smile.

"Of course, I know that," said Godfrey impatiently. "I'm not quite a fool."

"Not quite," repeated Andy emphasizing the last word in a way which made Godfrey color.

"What do you mean?" he said.

41

"What do I mane? It was only your words I repeated."

"Then, don't trouble yourself to repeat them -- do you hear?"

"Thank you. I won't."

"You didn't tell me whose gun that is."

"No, I didn't."

"Very likely you stole it," said Godfrey, provoked.

"Maybe you'll go and tell the owner."

"How can I when you haven't told me whose it is?"

"No more I did," said Andy with apparent innocence.

"Where are you going with it?"

"Goin' out shootin'."

"So I supposed."

"Did you, now? Then what made you ask?" returned Andy.

"You are an impudent fellow," said Godfrey, provoked.

"I never am impudent to gentlemen," said Andy pointedly.

Do you mean to say that I am not a gentleman?" demanded the other angrily.

"Suit yourself," said Andy coolly.

"You're only an Irish boy."

"Shure, I knew that before. Why can't you tell me some news? I'm an Irish boy and I'm proud of the same. I'll never go back on old Ireland."

"The Irish are a low set."

"Are they now? Maybe you never heard of Burke, the great orator."

"What of him?"

"Shure, he was an Irishman, and isn't my name Andy Burke, and wasn't he my great-grandfather?"

"He must be proud of his great-grandson," said Godfrey sarcastically.

"I never axed him, but no doubt you're right. But it's time I was goin', or I shan't get any birds. Would you like to come with me?"

"No, I am particular about the company I keep."

"I'm not, or I wouldn't have invited you," said Andy who was more quick witted than his opponent.

"I should like to know where he got that gun," said Godfrey to himself, following with his eyes the retreating figure of our hero. "I am sure that isn't his gun. Ten to one he stole it from somebody."

But Godfrey's curiosity was not destined to be gratified that afternoon, as it might have been if he had seen Andy turning into the yard of the Misses Grant two hours afterward. He had not shot anything, but he had got used to firing the gun and was now unlikely to be caught in any such adventure similar to the one in the last chapter.

CHAPTER X

ANDY'S DEBUT AT SCHOOL

The first of September came and with it came the opening of the fall schools. On the first day when Andy was at work in the yard and saw the boys and girls go by with their books, he felt a longing to go, too. He knew very well that his education had been much neglected and that he knew less of books than a boy of his age ought to do.

"I wish I could go to school this term," he said to himself, "but it's no use wishin'. Mother needs my wages, and I must keep on workin'."

The same thought had come to the Misses Grant. Andy had been in their employ now for six weeks, and by his unfailing good humor and readiness to oblige, he had won their favor. They felt interested in his progress, and at the same moment that the thought of school passed through Andy's mind, Miss Priscilla said to her sister, "The fall school begins today. There's Godfrey Preston who has just passed with some books under his arm."

"Just so."

"I suppose Andrew would like to be going to school with other boys of his age."

"Indeed."

"Don't you think we could spare him to go half the day?"

"Yes," said Sophia with alacrity.

"There isn't so much work to do now as there was in the summer, and he could do his chores early in the morning. He could go to school in the morning and work in the afternoon."

"Just so, Priscilla. Shall we give him less wages?"

"No, I think not. He needs the money to give his mother."

"Call him in and tell him," suggested Sophia.

"I will do so at lunch time."

"Just so."

When the lunch was over and Andy rose from the table, Miss Priscilla introduced the subject.

"Are you a good scholar, Andrew?"

"I'm a mighty poor one, ma'am."

"Did you ever study much?"

44

"No, ma'am. I've had to work ever since I was so high," indicating a point about two feet from the ground.

"Dear me," said Sophia, "you must have been very small."

"Yes, ma'am. I was very small in size."

"I've been thinking, Andrew, that perhaps we could spare you half the day so that you could go to school in the morning; you could learn something in three hours. Should you like it?"

"Would I like it, ma'am? Wouldn't I, though? I don't want to grow up a poor, ignorant crathur, hardly able to read and write."

"Then you can go to school tomorrow and ask the teacher if he will take you for half the day. You can get up early and get your chores done before school."

"Oh, yes, ma'am, I can do that easy."

"I think we have some schoolbooks in the house. Some years ago we had a nephew stay with us and go to school. I think his books are still in the closet."

"Thank you, ma'am. It'll save me buyin', and I haven't got any money to spare."

"We shall give you the same wages, Andrew, though you will work less."

"Thank you, ma'am. You're very kind."

"Try to improve your time in school, as becomes the great-grandson of such a distinguished orator."

I'll try, ma'am," said Andy, looking a little uneasy at this allusion to the great Edmund Burke. In fact, he was ashamed of having deceived the kind old ladies but didn't like now to own up to the deception lest they should lose confidence in him. But he determined hereafter to speak the truth and not resort to deception.

The next morning, at twenty minutes of nine, Andy left the house with his new books, and he joyfully took his way to the schoolhouse which was a quarter of a mile distant. As he ascended the small hill on which it stood, he attracted the attention of a group of boys who had already arrived. Among them was his old adversary, Godfrey Preston.

"Is that Irish boy coming to school?" he said in a tone of disgust.

"What? Andy Burke? I hope so," said Charles Fleming, "He's a good fellow."

"He's only an Irish boy," said Godfrey with a sneer.

"And I am only an American boy," said Charles good-humoredly.

"You can associate with him if you want to. I shan't," said Godfrey.

"That's where I agree with you, Godfrey," said Ben Travers, who made himself rather a toady of Godfrey's.

Andy had now come up, and so Charles Fleming did not reply but called out cordially, "Are you coming to school, Andy?"

"Yes," said Andy.

"I'm glad of it."

"Thank you," said Andy. "What's the matter with them fellows?" asked Andy as Godfrey and Ben Travers walked off haughtily, tossing their heads.

Charles Fleming laughed.

"They don't think we are good enough for their company," he said.

"I'm not anxious for it," said Andy. "I like yours better."

"I didn't think you could get away from work to come to school. Are you working for Miss Grant now?"

"Yes, but she lets me come to school half the day. She's a bully ould lady."

"Well, half a loaf's better than no bread. Will you sit with me? I've got no one at my desk. Say yes."

"It's just what I'd like, Charlie, but maybe Godfrey Preston wants to sit with me. I wouldn't like to disappoint him," said Andy with sly humor.

"Sit with me till he invites you, then."

"That'll be a long day."

They went into the schoolhouse, and Andy deposited his books in the desk next to Charlie Fleming's. He couldn't have wished for a better or more agreeable companion. Charlie was the son of Dr. Fleming, the village physician, and was a general favorite in the town on account of his sunny, attractive manner. But, with all his affability, he was independent and resolute if need be. He was one of the leaders of the school. Godfrey aspired also to be a leader -- and, to some extent, was, on account of his father's wealth and high standing, for, as we have seen, Colonel Preston was not like his son. He was too selfish in disposition and offensively consequential in manner to inspire devoted friendship. Ben Travers, however, flattered him and followed him about simply because he was the son of a rich man. Such cases occur sometimes among American schoolboys, but generally they are too democratic and sensible to attach importance to social distinctions in the schoolroom or on the playground.

A schoolboy carries his slate board and book.

When the teacher -- a certain Ebenezer Stone, a man of thirty or upward -- entered, Andy went up to him and asked permission to attend school part of the time. As there had been such cases in previous terms, no objection was offered by the teacher, and Andy went back to his seat as a regularly admitted member of the school.

It was found necessary to put him in a low class to begin with. He was naturally bright, but, as we know, his opportunities for learning had been very limited, and he could not be expected to know much. But Andy was old enough now to understand the worth of knowledge, and he devoted himself so earnestly to study that, in the course of three weeks, he was promoted to a higher class. This, however, is not surprising.

When recess came, the scholars poured out upon the playground. Charles Fleming and Godfrey Preston happened to pass out side by side.

"I see you've taken that Irish boy to sit with you," he said.

"You mean Andy Burke? Yes, I invited him to be my deskfellow."

"I congratulate you on your high-toned and aristocratic associate," observed Godfrey sarcastically.

"Thank you. I am glad to have him with me."

"I wouldn't condescend to take him into my seat."

"Nor do I. There isn't any condescension about it."

"He works for a living."

"So does my father, and so does yours. Are you going to cut your father's acquaintance for that reason?"

"My father could live without work."

"He doesn't choose to, and that's where he shows his good sense."

"It's a different kind of work from sawing and splitting wood and such low labor."

"It strikes me, Godfrey, that you ought to have been born somewhere else than in America. In this country labor is considered honorable. You ought to be living under a monarchy."

"I don't believe in associating with inferiors."

"I don't look upon Andy Burke as my inferior," said Charlie. "He is poor, to be sure, but he is a good fellow, and he helps support his mother and sister, as I would do in his place."

"Charlie Fleming," was heard from the playground, "come and split into teams for baseball."

Without waiting for an answer, Charlie ran to the field alongside the schoolhouse where the game was to take place.

CHAPTER XI

A GAME OF BALL

"Come here," said Conrad Fletcher. "Come here, Charlie, and split into teams for a game. We must make haste, or recess will be over."

"All right, Conrad."

The first choice devolved upon Conrad. He chose Ephraim Pinkham, known as a good catcher.

"I take Elmer Rhodes," said Charlie.

"John Parker," said Conrad.

"Henry Strauss."

"Godfrey Preston," was Conrad's next choice.

"Can you play, Andy?" asked Charlie.

"Yes," said Andy.

"Then, I take you."

"I've a good mind to resign," said Godfrey in a low voice to Ben Travers. "I don't fancy playing with that Irish boy."

However, he was too fond of playing to give up his place, notwithstanding his antipathy to Andy.

Charlie Fleming's side went in first, and Charlie himself went to the bat. The pitcher was Godfrey. He was really a fair pitcher, and he considered himself very superior. Charlie finally succeeded in hitting the ball but did so rather feebly, and he narrowly escaped losing his first base. He saved it, however.

Next at the bat was Elmer Rhodes. He hit one or two fouls, but not a fair ball. Finally he was put out on three strikes. Meanwhile, however, Charlie Fleming got round to third base. Henry Strauss succeeded in striking the ball, but it was caught by center field, rapidly sent to first base before Henry could reach it, and then thrown to the catcher in time to prevent Charlie Fleming from getting in. He ran halfway to home base, but seeing his danger ran back to third base. Next, Andy took the bat.

"Knock me in, Andy," called out Charlie Fleming.

"All right" said Andy quietly.

"Not if I can prevent it," said Godfrey to himself, and he determined -- by sending poor balls -- to get our hero out on three strikes. The first ball, therefore, he sent about six feet to the right of the batter. Andy stood in position, and, of course, was far too wise to attempt hitting any such ball. The next ball went several feet above his head. Of this, too, he took no notice. The third would have hit him if he had not dodged.

"Why don't you knock at the balls?" asked Godfrey.

"I will, when you give me better ones," said Andy coolly.

"I don't believe you know how to bat," said Godfrey with a sneer.

"I don't believe you know how to pitch," returned Andy.

"How's that?" sending another ball whizzing by his left ear.

"I want them waist-high," said Andy. "My waist is about two feet lower than my ears."

Godfrey now resolved to put in a ball waist-high so swiftly that Andy could not hit it; but Godfrey had never seen Andy play. Our hero had a wonderfully quick eye and steady hand, and he struck the ball with such force to left field that not only did Charlie Fleming get in without difficulty, but Andy himself made a home run.

"That's a splendid hit," exclaimed Charlie with enthusiasm. "I didn't think you could play so well."

"I've played before today," said Andy composedly. "I told you I would get you in, and I meant what I said."

Godfrey looked chagrined at the result. He meant to demonstrate that Andy was no player, but he had only contributed to his brilliant success, for had he not sent in so swift a ball, the knock would not have been so forcible.

As there were but six on a side, two outs were considered all out.

"Who will catch?" asked Charlie Fleming. "I want to pitch."

"I will," said Andy.

"All right! If you can catch as you can bat, we'll cut down their score."

Andy soon showed that he was no novice at catching. He rarely let a ball pass him. When Godfrey's turn came to bat, one was already out, and Andy determined to put Godfrey out if possible. One strike had been called when Godfrey struck a foul which was almost impossible to catch. But then Andy ran, made a bound into the air, and caught it -- a very brilliant piece of play by which Godfrey and his side were put out. The boys on both sides applauded, for it was a piece of brilliant fielding which not one of them was capable of. That is, all applauded but Godfrey. He threw down his bat spitefully and said to Fleming, "You didn't give me good pitches."

"I gave you much better than you gave Andy," said Charlie.

"That's so!" chimed in two other boys.

"I won't play any more," said Godfrey.

Just then the bell rang so that the game was brought to a close. Andy received the compliments of the boys on his brilliant playing. He received them modestly and admitted that he probably couldn't make such a catch again. It was very disagreeable to Godfrey to hear Andy praised. He was rather proud of his baseball-playing, and he saw that Andy was altogether his superior -- at any rate he was superior in the opinion of the boys. However, he ingeniously contrived to mingle a compliment with a sneer.

"You're more used to baseball than to books," he said.

"True for you," said Andy.

"You're a head taller than any of the boys in your class."

"I know that," said Andy. "I haven't been to school as much as you."

"I should be ashamed if I didn't know more."

"So you ought," said Andy, "for you've been to school all your life. I hope to know more soon."

"Anyway, you can play ball," said Charlie Fleming.

"I'd rather be a good scholar."

"I'll help you, if you want any help."

"Thank you, Charlie."

They had now entered the schoolroom, and Andy took up his book and studied hard. He was determined to rise to a higher class as soon as possible, for it was not agreeable to him to reflect that he was the oldest and largest boy in his present class.

"Very well," said the teacher when his recitation was over. "If you continue to recite in this way, you will soon be promoted."

"I'll do my best, sir," said Andy, who listened to these words with pleasure.

"I wish you were coming in the afternoon, too, Andy," said his friend, Charlie Fleming, as they walked home together.

"So do I, Charlie, but I must work for my mother."

"That's right, Andy. I'd do the same in your place. I haven't such foolish ideas about work as Godfrey Preston."

"He ain't very fond of me," said Andy laughing.

"No, nor of anybody else. He only likes Godfrey Preston."

"We got into a fight the first day I ever saw him."

"What was it about?"

"He called my mother names and hit me. So I knocked him flat."

"You served him right. He's disgustingly conceited. Nobody likes him."

"Ben Travers goes around with him all the time."

"Ben likes him because he is rich. If he should lose his property, you'd see how soon he would leave him. That isn't a friend worth having."

"I've got one consolation," said Andy laughing. "Nobody likes me for my money."

"But someone likes you for yourself, Andy," said Charlie.

"Who?"

"Myself, to be sure."

"And I like you as much, Charlie," said Andy warmly. "You're ten times as good a fellow as Godfrey."

"I hope so," said Charlie. "That isn't saying very much, Andy."

So the friendship was cemented, but it did not end there. Charlie spoke of Andy's good qualities at home, and some time afterward Andy was surprised by an invitation to spend the evening at Dr. Fleming's. He felt a little bashful but finally went -- and he was not at all sorry for so doing. The whole family was a delightful one, Andy was welcomed as a warm friend of Charlie's, and, in the pleasant atmosphere of the doctor's fireside, he quite forgot that there was one who looked down upon him as an inferior being.

Dr. Fleming had himself been a poor boy. By a lucky chance -- or Providence, rather -- he had been put on the path of obtaining an education, and he was not disposed now in his prosperity to forget his days of early struggle.

Andy found that in spite of the three hours taken up at school, he was able to do all that was required of him by the Misses Grant. They were glad to hear of his success at school and continued to pay him five dollars a week for his services. This money he regularly carried to his mother -- after paying for the new clothes of which he stood so much in need.

CHAPTER XII

A LITTLE DIFFICULTY

It has already been said that Godfrey Preston was a conceited and arrogant boy. He had a very high idea of his own importance and expected that others would acknowledge it, but he was not altogether successful. He would like to have had Andy Burke look up to him as a member of a superior class, and in that case he might have condescended to patronize him as a chieftain might in the case of a humble retainer. But Andy didn't want to be patronized by Godfrey. Andy never showed by his manner that he felt beneath him socially, and this greatly vexed Godfrey.

"His mother used to iron at our house," he said to Ben Travers one day, "but my mother discharged her. I don't see why the boys treat him as an equal. I won't, for my part."

"Of course, he isn't your equal," said the subservient Ben. "That's a good joke."

"He acts as if he were," said Godfrey discontentedly.

"It's only his impudence."

"You are right," said Godfrey, rather liking this explanation. "He is one of the most impudent boys I know. I wish my father would send me to a fashionable school where I shouldn't meet such fellows. That's the worst of these public schools -- you meet all sorts of persons in them."

"Of course you do."

"I suppose this Burke will be the lowest form of manual laborer when he is a man."

"While you are a member of Congress."

"Very likely," said Godfrey loftily, "and he will claim that he was an old schoolmate of mine. It is disgusting."

"Of course it is. However, we needn't notice him."

"I don't mean to."

But in the course of the next week there was an occurrence which compelled Godfrey to "notice" his detested schoolfellow.

Among the scholars was a very pleasant boy of twelve named Alfred Parker. He was the son of a poor widow and was universally liked for his amiable and obliging disposition. One morning before school, he was engaged in some game which required him to run. He accidentally ran against Godfrey, who was just coming up the hill, with considerable force. Now, it was very evident that it was wholly unintentional, but Godfrey was greatly incensed.

"What do you mean by that, you little scamp?" he exclaimed furiously.

"Excuse me, Godfrey. I didn't mean to run into you."

"That doesn't go down."

"Indeed, I didn't. I didn't see you."

"I can't help it. You ought to have been more careful. Take that, to make you more careful."

As he said this, he seized him by the collar and, tripping him, laid him flat on his back.

"For shame, Godfrey!" said another boy standing by, but as it was a small boy, Godfrey only answered, "If you say that again, I'll serve you the same way."

Alfred tried to get up, but Godfrey put his knee on his breast.

"Let me up, Godfrey," said Alfred piteously. "I can't breathe. You hurt me."

"I'll teach you to run into me," said the bully.

"I didn't mean to."

"I want to make sure of your not doing it again."

"Do let me up," said Alfred.

In return, Godfrey only pressed more heavily, and the little fellow began to cry. But help was near at hand. Andy Burke happened to come up the hill just then and saw what was going on. He had a natural chivalry that prompted him always to take the weaker side. But besides this, he liked Alfred for his good qualities and disliked Godfrey for his bad ones. He did not hesitate a moment, therefore, but ran up and, seizing Godfrey by the collar with a powerful grasp, jerked him on his back in the twinkling of an eye. Then, completely turning the tables, he put his knee on Godfrey's chest, and said, "Now, you know how it is yourself. How do you like it?"

"Let me up," demanded Godfrey furiously.

"That's what Alfred asked you to do," said Andy coolly. "Why didn't you do it?"

"Because I didn't choose," answered the prostrate boy, almost foaming at the mouth with rage and humiliation.

"Then I don't choose to let you up."

"You shall suffer for this," said Godfrey struggling, but in vain.

"Not from your hands. Oh, you needn't try so hard to get up. I can hold you here all day if I choose."

"You're a low Irish boy!"

"You're lower than I am just now," said Andy.

"Let me up."

"Why didn't you let Alfred up?"

"He ran against me."

"Did he mean to?"

"No, I didn't, Andy," said Alfred, who was standing near. "I told Godfrey so, but he threw me over and pressed on my chest so hard that it hurt me."

"In this way," said Andy, increasing the pressure on his prostrate enemy.

Godfrey renewed his struggles, but again in vain.

"Please let him up now, Andy," said Alfred generously.

"If he'll promise not to touch you any more, I will."

"I won't promise," said Godfrey. "I won't promise anything to a low beggar."

"Then you must feel the low beggar's knee," said Andy.

"You wouldn't have got me down if I had been looking. You got the advantage of me."

"Did I? Well, then, I'll give you a chance."

Andy rose to his feet, and Godfrey, relieved from the pressure, arose, too. No sooner was he up than he flew like an enraged tiger at our hero; but Andy was quite his equal in strength and, being cool, had the advantage.

The result was that in a few seconds he found himself once more on his back.

"You see," said Andy, "it isn't safe for you to attack me. I won't keep you down any longer, but if you touch Alfred again, I'll give you something worse."

Godfrey arose from the ground and shook his fist at Andy.

"I'll make you remember this," he said.

"I want you to remember it yourself," said Andy.

Godfrey didn't answer but made his way sullenly to the schoolroom.

56

"Thank you, Andy," said Alfred gratefully, "for saving me from Godfrey. He hurt me a good deal."

"He's a brute," said Andy warmly. "Don't be afraid of him, Alfred, but come and tell me if he touches you again. I'll give him something he won't like."

"You must be very strong, Andy," said the little boy admiringly. "You knocked him over just as easy."

Andy laughed.

"Did you ever know an Irish boy that couldn't fight?" he asked. "I'm better with my fists than with my brains, Alfred."

"That's because you never went to school much. You're getting on fast, Andy."

"I'm tryin', Alfred," he said. "It's a shame for a big boy like me not to know as much as a little boy like you."

"You'll soon get ahead of me, Andy."

Meanwhile Godfrey, feeling far from comfortable, had taken his place in school. He was outraged by the thought that Andy, whom he regarded as so much beneath him, should have had the audacity to throw him down and put his knees on his chest. It made him grind his teeth when he thought of it. What should he do about it? He wanted to be revenged in some way, and he meant to be.

Finally he decided to report Andy to the teacher and, if possible, induce him to punish him.

"The teacher knows that my father's a man of influence," he said to himself. "He will believe me before that ragamuffin. If he doesn't, I'll try to get him turned away."

When, therefore, the bell rang for recess and the rest of the scholars hurried to the playground, Godfrey lingered behind. He waited till all the boys were gone and then went up to the teacher.

"Well, Godfrey, what is it?" asked the master.

"Mr. Stone, I want to make a complaint against Andrew Burke," said Godfrey.

"What has he done?"

"He is a brute," said Godfrey in an excited manner. "He dared to come up behind my back before school began and knock me down. Then he put his knee on my chest and wouldn't let me up."

"What made him do it?"

"He knows I don't like him and am not willing to associate with him."

"Was that all the reason?" asked the teacher keenly.

"I suppose so," said Godfrey.

"I was not aware that Andy Burke was quarrelsome," said the teacher. "He behaves well in school."

"Because he knows he must."

"Very well. I will inquire into the matter after recess."

Godfrey went back to his seat, triumphant. He didn't doubt that his enemy would be severely punished.

CHAPTER XIII

GODFREY'S REBELLION

Having made his complaint, Godfrey waited impatiently for the recess to close in order that he might see retribution fall upon the head of Andy. He had not long to wait. Meanwhile, however, he was missed in the playground.

"Where's Godfrey?" asked one of the boys.

"He don't want to come out. He got a licking from Andy Burke."

"I ain't much sorry. It'll cure him of some of his airs."

"I don't know about that. It comes natural to him to put on airs."

"If anybody has insulted Godfrey," remarked Ben Travers, Godfrey's toady, "he had better look out for himself."

"Do you hear that, Andy? Ben Travers says you must look out for yourself."

"Who's goin' to punish me?" asked Andy. "If it's Ben, let him come on."

But Ben showed no disposition to "come on." He could talk and threaten, but when words were to be succeeded by blows he never was on hand. In fact he was a coward and ought to have kept quiet, but it is just that class that are usually most noisy.

Andy had no idea that Godfrey would complain to the teacher in a matter where he was so clearly in the wrong, nor would Godfrey do so if he had not relied upon his father's position to carry him through.

"Mr. Stone is a poor man," he thought, "and he won't dare to take the part of a low Irish boy against the only son and heir of Colonel Preston. He knows on which side his bread is buttered, and he won't be such a fool as to offend my father."

While he said this he knew that it was very doubtful whether his father would espouse his cause, but then Mr. Stone would probably suppose he would, which would answer the same purpose on the present occasion.

When Andy re-entered the schoolroom with the rest of the boys at the termination of recess, he saw Godfrey in his seat. The latter darted a glance of malicious triumph at Andy.

When the noise of entering was over, Mr. Stone said, "Andrew Burke, come forward!"

Considerably surprised, Andy came forward and looked up with a modest self-possession into the teacher's face.

"A complaint has been entered against you, Andrew," Mr. Stone began.

"What is it, sir?" asked Andy.

"You are charged by Godfrey Preston with violently assaulting and throwing him down, just before school commenced. Is this true?"

"Yes, sir," answered Andy promptly.

"You are charged with kneeling down upon him and preventing him from getting up."

"That is true," said Andy quite composedly.

"I am surprised that you should have acted in this manner," said Mr. Stone. "I did not think you quarrelsome or a bully."

"I hope I am not," said Andy. "Did Godfrey tell you why I knocked him over?"

"He said it was because he would not associate with you."

Andy laughed.

"I hope you'll excuse my laughing, sir," he said respectfully, "but I'd rather associate with any of the other boys than with Godfrey. I like him least of all."

"Then, that is the reason you attacked him, is it?"

"No, sir."

"Then, what was it?"

"If you don't mind, sir, I'd like to have you ask Alfred Parker."

"Alfred Parker," called out the teacher, "Come forward."

Alfred obeyed.

"Do you know why Andrew attacked Godfrey Preston?"

"Yes, sir. It was on my account."

"On your account! Explain."

"This morning, before school, I was playing with another boy, and I accidentally ran into Godfrey. He got mad and threw me over violently. Then he pressed his knee on my chest till I could hardly breathe. I begged him to let me up, but he would not, though he knew that it was only an accident. While I was lying on the ground, Andy Burke came up. He no sooner saw me then he ran up, threw Godfrey off, and got on him in the same manner, and I think he served him right."

As he uttered these last words, Godfrey scowled ominously, but Andy's face brightened up. He was glad that Alfred was brave enough to speak up for him.

"This alters the case considerably," said the teacher. "Is there any other boy who witnessed the affair and can substantiate what has been said? If so, let him raise his hand."

Herman Reynolds raised his hand.

"Well, Herman, what do you know about it? Were you present?"

"Yes, sir, I was. It was just as Alfred said it was."

"What have you to say, Godfrey?" asked Mr. Stone sternly.

"I don't mean to be insulted by an Irish boy," said Godfrey haughtily.

"Remember where you are, sir, and speak in a more becoming manner. Did you attack Alfred Parker, as he says?"

"He had no business to run into me."

"Answer my question."

"Yes, I did."

"And did you kneel on his chest?"

"Yes."

"Oblige me by saying, 'Yes, sir.'"

"Yes, sir," said Godfrey reluctantly.

"Why do you complain, then, of being treated in a similar manner by Andrew?"

"He has no business to touch me."

"If he had not interfered when he saw you maltreating his young schoolfellow, I should have been ashamed of him," said the teacher.

This rang so true with the sentiment of the boys that they almost involuntarily applauded, and one boy, arising, exclaimed, "Three cheers for the teacher!"

The three cheers were given with a will, and though they were -- strictly speaking -- out of order, Mr. Stone was a sensible man, and the only notice he took of it was to say, "Thank you, boys. I am glad to find that you agree with me on this point and that your sympathies are with the weak and oppressed. Godfrey Preston, your complaint is dismissed. I advise you to cease acting the part of a bully, or you may get another similar lesson. Andrew, when you exert your strength, I hope it will always be in as just a cause. You may take your seat, and you also, Alfred."

The boys would have applauded again, but Mr. Stone said, waving his hand, "Once is enough, boys. Time is precious, and we must now go on with our lessons. First class is arithmetic."

Godfrey had been equally surprised and angry at the turn that affairs had taken. He was boiling with indignation and nervously moved about in his seat. After a slight pause, having apparently taken his determination, he took his cap and walked toward the door.

Mr. Stone's attention was drawn to him.

"Where are you going, Godfrey?" he demanded quickly.

"Home," said Godfrey.

"You will wait till the end of school."

"I would rather not, sir."

"It makes no difference what you would rather do or rather not do. Are you sick?"

"No, sir."

"Then you have no good cause for leaving, and I shall not permit you to do so."

"I have been insulted, sir, and I don't wish to stay."

"By whom?" demanded the teacher sharply.

Godfrey would like to have said, "By you," but he saw the teacher's keen eye fixed upon him, and he didn't dare to do it. He hesitated.

"By whom?" repeated Mr. Stone.

"By Andrew Burke."

"That is no good reason for your leaving school, or it would not be if it were true, but it is not. He has only meted out to you the same punishment you undertook to inflict upon a smaller boy. Take your seat."

"My father will take me away from school," said Godfrey angrily.

"We shall none of us mourn for your absence. Take your seat."

This last remark of the teacher still further incensed Godfrey and led him temporarily to forget himself. Though he had been bidden to take his seat, he resolved to leave the schoolroom and made a rush for the door. But Mr. Stone was there before him. He seized Godfrey by the collar and dragged him, shaking him as he proceeded, to his seat, on which he placed him with some emphasis.

"That is the way I treat rebels," he said. "You forget yourself, Preston. The next time you make up your mind to resist my commands, count in advance on a much more severe lesson."

Godfrey was pale with passion, and his hands twitched convulsively. He only wished he had Mr. Stone in his power for five minutes. He would treat him worse than he did Alfred Parker. But a boy in a rage is not a very pleasant spectacle. It is enough to say that Godfrey was compelled to stay in school for the remainder of the morning. As soon as he could get away, he ran home, determined to enlist his mother in his cause.

CHAPTER XIV

MR. STONE IS CALLED TO ACCOUNT

At home Godfrey gave a highly colored narrative of the outrageous manner in which he had been abused, as he chose to represent it. He gave this account to his mother, for his father was not at home. Indeed, he was absent for a day or two in a distant city.

Mrs. Preston was indignant.

"It is an outrage, Godfrey," she said, compressing her thin lips. "How did Mr. Stone dare to treat you in this way?"

"I was surprised, myself," said Godfrey.

"Had he no more respect for your father's prominent position?"

"It looks as if he didn't."

"He is evidently unfit to keep the school. I shall try to persuade your father to have him turned away."

"I wish he might be," said Godfrey. "It would teach him to treat me with proper respect. Anybody would think that Irish boy was the son of the most important man in town."

Both Godfrey and his mother appeared to take it for granted that a teacher should treat his pupils according to their social position. This is certainly very far from proper, as all my youthful readers will, I hope, agree.

"I don't want to go back to school this afternoon, mother," said Godfrey.

"I don't wonder," said his mother. "I will tell you what I will do. I will send a letter with you to Mr. Stone asking him to call here this evening. I will then take occasion to express my opinion of his conduct."

"That's good, mother," said Godfrey joyfully.

He knew that his mother had a sharp tongue, and he longed to hear his mother "give it" to the teacher whom he hated.

"Then, you think I had better go to school this afternoon?"

"Yes, with the note. If Mr. Stone does not apologize, you need not go tomorrow. I will go upstairs and write it at once."

The note was quickly written and, putting it carefully in his inside pocket, Godfrey went to school. As he entered the schoolroom he stepped up to the desk and handed the note to Mr. Stone.

"Here is a note from my mother," he said superciliously.

"Very well," said the teacher taking it gravely.

As it was not quite time to summon the pupils, he opened it at once.

This was what he read:

MR. STONE:

Sir -- My son Godfrey informs me that you have treated him in a very unjust manner, for which I find it impossible to account. I shall be glad if you can find time to call at my house this evening, in order that I may hear from your lips an explanation of the occurrence.

Yours, in haste,

Lucinda Preston.

"Preston," said Mr. Stone after reading this note, "you may say to your mother that I will call this evening."

He did not appear in the least disturbed by the contents of the note that he had received from the richest and -- in her own eyes -- the most important lady in the village. In fact, he had a large share of self-respect and independence and was not likely to submit to browbeating from anyone. He tried to be just in his treatment of the scholars under his charge, and if he ever failed, it was from misunderstanding or ignorance, not from design. In the present instance he felt that he had done right and resolved to maintain the justice of his conduct.

Nothing of importance occurred in the afternoon. Godfrey was very quiet and orderly. He felt that he could afford to wait. With malicious joy, he looked forward to the scolding Mr. Stone was to get from his mother.

"He won't dare to talk to her," he said to himself. "I hope she'll make him apologize to me. He ought to do it before the school."

Evidently Godfrey had a very inadequate idea of the teacher's pluck if he thought such a thing possible.

School was dismissed, and Godfrey went home. He dropped a hint to Ben Travers that his mother was going to "haul Mr. Stone over the coals," as he expressed it.

"Are you going to be there?" asked Ben when Godfrey had finished.

"Yes," said Godfrey. "It'll be my turn then."

"Perhaps Mr. Stone will have something to say," said Ben doubtfully.

"He won't dare to," said Godfrey confidently. "He knows my father could get him kicked out of school."

"He's rather spunky, the master is," said Ben, who, toady as he was, understood the character of Mr. Stone considerably better than Godfrey did.

"I'll tell you all about it tomorrow morning," said Godfrey.

"All right."

"I expect he'll apologize to me for what he did."

"Maybe he will," answered Ben, but he thought it highly improbable.

"Did you give my note to Mr. Stone?" asked his mother.

"Yes."

"What did he say?"

"He said he'd come around."

"How did he appear?"

"He looked a little nervous," said Godfrey, speaking not according to facts, but according to his wishes.

"I thought so," said Mrs. Preston with a look of satisfaction. "He will find that he has made a mistake in treating you so outrageously."

"Give it to him right and left, mother," said Godfrey with more force than elegance.

"You might express yourself more properly, my son," said Mrs. Preston. "I shall endeavor to impress upon his mind the impropriety of his conduct."

At half-past seven, Mr. Stone rang the bell at Mrs. Preston's door and was ushered in without delay.

"Good evening, Mrs. Preston," he said bowing. "Your son brought me a note this afternoon requesting me to call. I have complied with your request."

"Be seated, Mr. Stone," said the lady frigidly, not offering her hand.

"Thank you," said the teacher with equal ceremony, and he did as invited.

"I suppose you can guess the object of my request," said Mrs. Preston.

"I think you stated it in your note."

"I desire an explanation of the manner in which you treated my son this morning, Mr. Stone."

"Pardon me, madam; your son is in the room."

"Well, sir?"

"I decline discussing the matter before him."

"I cannot understand why you should object to his presence."

66

"I am his teacher, and he is subject to my authority. You apparently desire to find fault with the manner in which I have exercised that authority. It is improper that the discussion upon this point should take place before him."

"May I stay in the room, mother?" asked Godfrey, who was alarmed lest he should miss the spectacle of Mr. Stone's humiliation.

"I really don't see why not," returned his mother.

"Madam," said Mr. Stone rising, "I will bid you good evening."

"What, sir; before we have spoken on the subject?"

"I distinctly decline to speak before your son for the reasons already given."

"This is very singular, sir. However, I will humor your whims. Godfrey, you may leave the room."

"Can't I stay?"

"I am compelled to send you out."

Godfrey went out, though with a very ill grace.

"Now, madam," said the teacher, "I have no objection to telling you that I first reprimanded your son for brutal treatment of a younger schoolmate and then forcibly carried him back to his seat when he endeavored to leave the schoolroom without my permission."

It was Mrs. Preston's turn to be surprised. She had expected to overawe the teacher, and instead of that she found him firmly and independently defending his course.

"Mr. Stone," she said, "my son tells me that you praised an Irish boy in your school for a violent and brutal assault which he made upon him."

"I did not praise him for that. I praised him for promptly interfering to prevent Godfrey from abusing a boy smaller and younger than himself."

"Godfrey had good cause for punishing the boy you refer to. He acted in self-defense."

"He has doubtless misrepresented the affair to you, madam, as he did to me."

"You take this Andrew Burke's word against his?"

"I form my judgment upon the testimony of an eyewitness and from what I know of your son's character."

"From your own statement, this low Irish boy -- "

"To whom do you refer, madam?"

"To the Irish boy."

"I have yet to learn that he is low."

"Do you mean to compare him with my son?"

"In wealth, no. Otherwise, you mustn't blame me for saying that I hold him entirely equal in respectability and, in some important points, his superior."

"Really, sir, your language is most extraordinary."

At this moment there was an interruption. Godfrey had been listening at the keyhole but, finding that difficult, had opened the door slightly; however, in his interest Godfrey managed to stumble against it. The door flew open, and he fell forward upon his knees on the carpet of the sitting room.

CHAPTER XV

MRS. PRESTON'S DISCOMFITURE

Godfrey rose to his feet, red with mortification. His mother looked disconcerted. Mr. Stone said nothing but glanced significantly from Godfrey to Mrs. Preston.

"What is the matter, Godfrey?" she asked rather sharply.

"It was an accident," said Godfrey rather sheepishly.

"You can go out and shut the door, and take care not to let such an accident happen again. For some unknown reason, Mr. Stone prefers that you should not be present, and, therefore, you must go."

For once, Godfrey found nothing to say but withdrew in silence.

"You appear to have formed a prejudice against Godfrey, Mr. Stone," said Mrs. Preston.

"I may have formed an unfavorable judgment of him on some points," said the teacher. "I judge him by his conduct."

"To say that Andrew Burke is his superior is insulting to him and his family, as well as ludicrous."

"I beg pardon, Mrs. Preston, but I must dissent from both your statements. Andrew Burke possesses some excellent qualities in which Godfrey is deficient."

"He is a poor working boy."

"He is none the worse for that."

"He should remember his position and treat my son with proper respect."

"I venture to say that Godfrey will receive all the respect to which he is entitled. May I ask if you expect him to be treated with deference because his father is richer than those of the other boys?"

"It seems to me only proper."

"Do you expect me to treat him any better on that account?"

"I think my son's social position should command respect."

"Then, Mrs. Preston, I entirely disagree with you," said Mr. Stone firmly. "As a teacher I have nothing whatsoever to do with the social position of the children who come to me as pupils. From me, a poor boy will receive the same instruction, and the same treatment precisely, as the son of rich parents. If he behaves as he should, he will always find in me a friend, as well as a teacher. Your son Godfrey shall have no just complaint to make of my treatment. I will give him credit for good conduct and faithful study but no more than

---

to Andrew Burke, or to any other pupil under the same circumstances."

"Mr. Stone, I am surprised at your singular style of talking. You wish to do away with all social distinctions."

"I certainly do, madam, in my schoolroom at least. There must be social differences, I am aware. We cannot all be equally rich or honored, but whatever may be the world's rule, I mean to maintain strict impartiality in my classroom."

"Will you require Andy Burke to apologize to Godfrey?"

"Why should I?"

"For his violent assault upon him."

"Certainly not. He was justified in his conduct."

"If my son was doing wrong, the Irish boy, instead of interfering, should have waited till you came and then reported the matter to you."

"And, meanwhile, stood by and seen Alfred Parker inhumanely treated?"

"I presume the matter has been greatly exaggerated."

"I do not, madam."

"Do I understand that you decline to make reparation to my son?"

"Reparation for what?"

"For the manner in which he has been treated."

"I must have talked to little purpose, if I have not made it clear that your son has only received his deserts. Of course, he is entitled to no reparation, as you term it."

"Then, Mr. Stone," said Mrs. Preston, her thin lips compressed with indignation, "since Godfrey cannot meet with fair treatment, I shall be compelled to withdraw him from your school."

"That must be as you please, madam," said the teacher, quite unmoved by the threatened withdrawal of his richest pupil.

"I shall report to Colonel Preston your treatment of his son."

"I have no objection, madam."

"You are pursuing a very unwise course in alienating your wealthiest patrons."

"I have no patrons, madam," said Mr. Stone proudly. "I return faithful service for the moderate wages I receive, and the obligation, if there is any, is on the part of those whose children I instruct."

"Really," thought Mrs. Preston, "this man is very independent for a poor teacher."

She resolved upon another shot, not in the best of taste.

"You must not be surprised, Mr. Stone," she said, "if the school trustees refuse to employ you again."

"You mistake me utterly," said the teacher with dignity, "if you suppose that any such threat or consideration will make me swerve from my duty. However, though I did not propose to mention it, I will state that this is the last term I shall teach in this village. I have been engaged at double the salary in a neighboring city."

Mrs. Preston was disappointed to hear this. It was certainly vexatious that the man who had treated her son with so little consideration, who had actually taken the part of a working boy against him, should be promoted to a better position. She had thought to make him feel that he was in her power, but she now saw that her anticipations were not to be realized.

As she did not speak, Mr. Stone considered the interview closed, and he rose.

"Good evening, Mrs. Preston," he said.

"Good evening, sir," she responded coldly.

He bowed and withdrew.

When Godfrey, who was not far off -- though he had thought it best not to play the part of eavesdropper again -- heard the door close, he hurried into the room.

"Well, mother, what did he say?" he inquired eagerly.

"He obstinately refused to make any reparation to you."

"Did you tell him what you thought of his treatment of me?" said Godfrey, rather surprised that his mother's remonstrance had produced no greater effect.

"Yes, I expressed my opinion very plainly. I must say that he's a very impudent man. The idea of a poor teacher putting on such airs!" continued Mrs. Preston tossing her head.

"What did he say?"

"That that Irish boy was superior to you."

"I'd like to knock him over," said Godfrey wrathfully.

Mrs. Preston was a lady, and it is not to be supposed that she should join in her son's wish. Still, it did not occur to her that she should mourn very much if Mr. Stone met with a reverse. She would like to see his pride humbled, not reflecting that her own was greater and less justifiable.

"You ought to have told him that he would lose his school," said Godfrey. "That would have frightened him, for he is a poor man and depends on the money he gets for teaching."

"He is not going to teach here after this term."

"Good! Did he tell you that?"

"Yes."

"He is afraid of me, after all."

"You are mistaken, Godfrey. He is offered considerably higher pay in another place."

Godfrey's countenance fell. It was as disagreeable to him as to his mother to learn that Mr. Stone was to be promoted in his profession.

"Shall I have to go to school again, mother?" he asked after a pause.

"No," said Mrs. Preston with energy. "Upon that I am determined. While Mr. Stone is teacher, you shall not go back. I will take care to let it be known in the neighborhood why I keep you at home. I hope the next teacher will be a man who understands the respect due to social position. I don't care to have you put on an equality with such boys as Andrew Burke. He is no fit associate for you."

"That is what I think, mother," said Godfrey. "The low beggar! I'd like to come up with him. Perhaps, I shall have a chance some day."

When Colonel Preston returned home, the whole story was told to him, but -- colored though it was -- he guessed how matters actually stood and was far from becoming his son's partisan. He privately went to Mr. Stone and obtained his version of the affair.

"You did right, Mr. Stone," he said at the end. "If my son chooses to act the bully, he must take the consequences. Mrs. Preston does not look upon it in the same light and insists upon my taking Godfrey from school. For the sake of peace, I must do so, but you must not construe it as showing any disapproval on my part of your course in the matter."

"Thank you, Colonel Preston," said the teacher warmly. "I can only regret Mrs. Preston's displeasure. Your approval I highly value, and it will encourage me in the path of duty."

CHAPTER XVI

THE CHRISTMAS PRESENT

Godfrey didn't return to school at all. He fancied that it would be more aristocratic to go to a boarding school; his mother concurred in this view, and he was entered as a scholar at the Melville Academy, situated in Melville twelve miles distant. Once a fortnight he came home to spend the Sunday. On these occasions he flourished about with a tiny cane and put on more airs than ever. No one outside of his own family missed him much. Andy found the school considerably more agreeable after his departure.

Twelve months passed. During this time Andy grew considerably and was now quite a stout boy. He also improved in education. The Misses Grant, taking a kind interest in his progress, managed to spare him half the day in succeeding terms so that he continued to attend school. Knowing that he had but three hours to learn, when the others had six, he was all the more diligent and was quite up to the average standard for boys of his age. The fact is, Andy was an observing boy, and he realized that education was essential to success in life. Before going away Mr. Stone talked with him on this subject and gave him some advice, which Andy determined to follow.

As may be inferred from what I have said, Andy was still working for the Misses Grant. He had grown accustomed to their ways and succeeded in giving them perfect satisfaction; he accomplished quite as much work as John, his predecessor, even though the latter was a grown man.

As Christmas approached, Miss Priscilla said one day to her sister, "Don't you think, Sophia, it would be well to give Andrew a Christmas present?"

"Just so," returned Sophia approvingly.

"He has been very faithful and obliging all the time he has been with us."

"Just so."

"I have been thinking what would be a good thing to give him."

"A pair of spectacles," suggested Sophia rather absent-mindedly.

"Sophia, you are a goose."

"Just so," acquiesced her sister meekly.

"Such a gift would be very inappropriate."

"Right."

"A pair of boots," was the next suggestion.

"That would be better. Boots would be very useful, but I think it would be well to give him something that would contribute to his amusement. Of course, we must consult his taste and not our own. We are not boys."

"Just so," said Sophia promptly. "And he is not a lady," she added enlarging upon the idea.

"Of course not. Now, the question is, what do boys like?"

"Just so," said Sophia, but this admission did not throw much light upon the character of the present to be bought.

Just then Andy himself helped them to a decision. He entered, cap in hand, and said, "If you can spare me, Miss Grant, I would like to go skating on the pond."

"Have you a pair of skates, Andrew?"

"No, ma'am," said Andy, "but one of the boys will lend me a pair."

"Yes, Andrew; you can go if you will be home early."

"Yes, ma'am. Thank you."

As he went out, Miss Priscilla said, "I have it."

"What?" asked Sophia alarmed.

"I mean that I have found out what to give to Andrew."

"What is it?"

"A pair of skates."

"Just so," said Sophia. "He will like them."

"So I think. Suppose we go to the store while he is away and buy him a pair."

"Won't he need to try them on?" asked her sister.

"No," said Priscilla. "They don't need to fit as exactly as boots."

So the two sisters made their way to the village store and asked to look at their stock of skates.

"Are you going to skate, Miss Priscilla?" asked the shopkeeper jocosely.

"No, they are for Sophia," answered Priscilla, who could joke occasionally.

"Oh, Priscilla," answered the matter-of-fact Sophia, "you didn't tell me about that. I am sure I could not skate. You said they were for Andrew."

"Sophia, you are a goose."

"Just so."

"It was only a joke."

"Oh."

The ladies, who never did things half-heartidly selected the best pair in the store and paid for them. When Andy had returned from skating, Priscilla asked, "How did you like the skating, Andrew?"

"It was bully," said Andrew enthusiastically.

"Whose skates did you borrow?"

"Alfred Parker's. They were too small for me, but I made them do."

"I should suppose you would like to have a pair of your own."

"So I should, but I can't afford to buy a pair, just yet. I'll tell you what I want to do, and maybe you'll help me about buyin' it."

"What is it, Andrew?"

"You know Christmas is comin', ma'am, and I want to buy my mother a nice dress for a Christmas present -- not a calico one but a thick one for winter."

"Alpaca or de laine?"

"I expect so. I don't know the name of what I want, but you do. How much would it cost?"

"I think you could get a good de laine for fifty cents a yard. I saw some at the store this afternoon."

"And about how many yards would be wanted, ma'am?"

"About twelve, I should think."

"Then it would be six dollars."

"Just so," said Sophia, who thought it about time she took part in the conversation.

"I've got the money, ma'am, and I'll give it to you, if you and Miss Sophia will be kind enough to buy it for me."

"To be sure we will, Andrew," said Priscilla kindly. "I am glad you are such a good son."

"Just so, Andrew."

"You see," said Andy, "mother won't buy anything for herself. She always wants to buy things for Mary and me. She wants us to be well-dressed, but she goes with the same old clothes. So I want her to have a new dress."

"You want her to have it at Christmas, then?"

"Yes, ma'am, if it won't be too much trouble."

"That is in two days. Tomorrow Sophia and I will buy the dress."

"Thank you. Here's the money," and Andy counted out six dollars in bills, of which Miss Priscilla took charge.

The next day they fulfilled their commission and purchased a fine dress pattern at the village store. It cost rather more than six dollars, but this they paid out of their own pockets and did not report to Andy. Just after supper, as he was about to go home to spend Christmas Eve, they placed the bundle in his hands.

"Isn't it beautiful!" he exclaimed with delight. "Won't mother be glad to get it?"

"She'll think she has a good son, Andrew."

"Shure, I ought to be good to her for she's a jewel of a mother."

"That is right, Andrew. I always like to hear a boy speak well of his mother. It is a great pleasure to a mother to have a good son."

"Shure, ma'am," said Andy with more kindness of heart than discretion, "I hope you'll have one yourself."

"Just so," said Sophia with the forced habit upon her.

"Sophia, you are a goose!" said Priscilla blushing a little.

"Just so, Priscilla."

"We are too old to marry, Andrew," said Priscilla, "but we thank you for your wish."

"Shure, ma'am, you are only in the prime of life."

"Indeed," said Sophia brightening up.

"I shall be sixty next spring. That can hardly be in the prime of life."

"I was readin' of a lady that got married at seventy-nine, ma'am."

"Oh," said Sophia eagerly.

Miss Priscilla did not care to pursue the subject.

"We have thought of you," she continued, "and, as you have been very obliging, we have bought you a Christmas present. Here it is."

Andy no sooner saw the skates than his face brightened up with the most evident satisfaction.

"It's just what I wanted," he said joyfully. "They're regular beauties! I'm ever so much obliged to you."

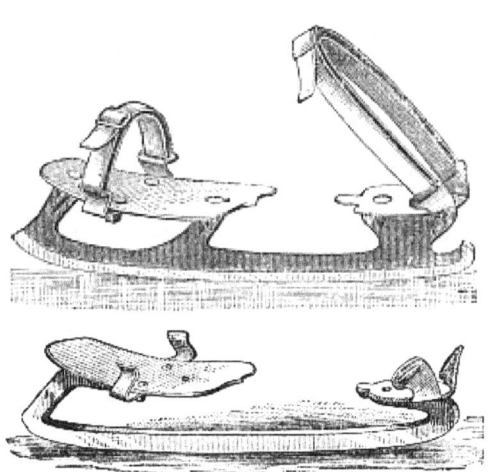

**Ice skates from the late 1870's were made to
strap over children's shoes or boots.**

"Sophia wanted to get you a pair of spectacles, but I thought these would suit you better."

Andy went off into a fit of laughter at the idea, in which both the ladies joined him. Then, after thanking them again, he hurried home, hardly knowing which gave him greater pleasure -- his own present or his mother's.

I will not stop to describe Andy's Christmas but will carry my reader forward to the next September when Andy met with an adventure, an adventure which eventually had a considerable effect upon his fortunes.

CHAPTER XVII

INTRODUCES A CONMAN

Colonel Preston, as I have already said, was a rich man. He owned no real estate in the town of Crampton except for the house in which he lived. His property was chiefly in stocks of different kinds. Included in these was a considerable amount of stock in a woolen manufacturing establishment, situated in Melville some twelve miles distant. Dividends upon these were paid semi-annually on the first of April and October. It was the custom of Colonel Preston at these dates to drive over to Melville, receive his dividends, and then drive back again.

Now, unfortunately for the welfare of the community, there are some persons who, unwilling to make a living by honest industry, prefer to possess themselves by unlawful means to maintain their unprofitable lives. Among them was a certain black-whiskered individual who, finding himself too well known in New York, had sought the country and was ready for any stroke of business which might arise in his particular line. Chance led his steps to Melville where he checked in at the village inn. He began at once to institute inquiries, the answers to which might serve his purpose; to avert suspicion, he casually mentioned that he was a capitalist and thought of settling down in the town. As he was well dressed and had a plausible manner, this statement was not doubted.

Among other things, he made inquiries in regard to the manufactory -- what dividends it paid and when. Expressing himself desirous of purchasing some stock, he inquired the names of the principal owners of the stock. First among them mentioned was Colonel Preston.

"Perhaps he might sell some stocks," suggested the landlord.
"Where can I see him?" asked James Fairfax, for this was the name assumed by the conman.

"You can see him here," answered the landlord, "in a day or two. He will be here the first of the month to receive his dividends."

"Will he stay with you?"

"Probably. He generally dines with me when he comes over."

"Will you introduce me?"

"With pleasure."

Mr. Fairfax appeared to hear this with satisfaction and said that he would make Colonel Preston an offer for a part of his stock.

"Most of my property is invested in real estate in New York," he said, "but I should like to have some manufacturing stock, and, from what you tell me, I think favorably of the Melville Mills."

"We should be glad to have you settle down among us," said the landlord.

"I shall probably do so," said Fairfax. "I am very much pleased with your town and people."

In due time Colonel Preston drove over. As usual, he stayed at the hotel.

"Colonel," said the landlord, "there's a gentleman stopping with me who desires an introduction to you."

"Indeed! What is his name?"

"James Fairfax."

"Is he from this neighborhood?"

"No, from the city of New York."

"I shall be happy to make his acquaintance," said the colonel courteously, "but it must be after I return from the mills. I shall be there a couple of hours, probably. We are to have a directorial meeting."

"I will tell him."

Colonel Preston attended the directors' meeting and also collected his dividend, amounting to eight hundred dollars. These, in eight one-hundred-dollar bills, he put in his wallet and then returned to the hotel for lunch.

"Lunch is not quite ready, colonel," said the landlord. "It will be ready in fifteen minutes."

"Where is the gentleman who wished to be introduced to me?" asked Colonel Preston, who thought it would save time to be introduced now. "I will speak to him."

He went directly to a dark-complexioned man with black whiskers and eyes that were rather sinister in appearance. The eyes oftenest betray the real character of a man, where all other signs fail. But Colonel Preston was not a keen observer, nor was he skilled in physiognomy, and, judging Mr. Fairfax merely by his manner, he was rather pleased with him.

"You will pardon my obtruding myself upon you, Colonel Preston," said the stranger with great ease of manner.

I am happy to make your acquaintance, sir."

"I am a stranger in this neighborhood. The city of New York is my home. I have been led here by the recommendations of friends who knew that I desired to locate myself in the country."

"How do you like Melville?"

"Very much -- so much that I may settle down here. But, Colonel Preston, I am a man of business, and if I am to be here, I want some local interest -- some stake in the town itself."

"Quite natural, sir."

"You are a businessman yourself and will understand me. Now, to come to the point, I find you have a manufactory here -- a woolen manufactory -- which I am given to understand is prosperous and profitable."

"You are correctly informed, Mr. Fairfax. It is paying twelve per cent dividends, and it has done so for several years."

"That is excellent. It is a better rate than I get for most of my city investments."

"I also have city investments -- bank stocks and horse-railroad stocks -- but, as you say, my mill stock pays me better than the majority of these."

"You are a large owner of the mill stock, are you not, Colonel Preston?"

"Yes, sir. The largest, I believe."

"So I am informed. Would you be willing to part with any of it?"

"I have never thought of doing so. I am afraid I could not replace it with any other that would be satisfactory."

"I don't blame you, of course, but it occurred to me that, having a considerable amount, you might be willing to sell."

"I generally hold on to good stock when I get possession of it. Indeed, I would buy more, if there were any in the market."

"He must have surplus funds," thought the conman. "I must see if I can't manage to get some into my possession."

Here the landlord appeared and announced that lunch was ready.

"You dine here, then?" said Fairfax.

"Yes. It will take me two hours to reach home, so I am obliged to dine here."

"We shall dine together, it seems. I am glad of it, as at present I happen to be the only permanent guest at the hotel. May I ask where you live?"

"In Crampton."

"I have heard favorably of it and have been intending to come over and see the place, but the fact is, I am used only to the city, and your country roads are so blind that I have been afraid of losing my way."

"Won't you ride over with me this afternoon, Mr. Fairfax? I can't bring you back, but you are quite welcome to a seat in my coach one way."

The eyes of the highwayman sparkled at the invitation. Colonel Preston had fallen into the trap he had laid for him, but he thought it best not to accept too eagerly.

"You are certainly very kind, Colonel Preston," he answered, with affected hesitation, "but I am afraid I shall be troubling you too much."

"No trouble whatever," said Colonel Preston heartily. "It is a lonely ride, and I shall be glad of a companion."

"A lonely ride, is it?" thought Fairfax. "All the better for my purpose. It shall not be my fault if I do not come back with my pockets well lined. The dividends you have just collected will be better in my pockets than in yours."

This was what Fairfax thought, but he said, "Then I will accept with pleasure. I suppose I can easily engage someone to bring me back to Melville?"

"Oh, yes. We have a livery stable where you can easily obtain a horse and driver."

The lunch proceeded, and Fairfax made himself unusually social and agreeable so that Colonel Preston congratulated himself on the prospect of beguiling the loneliness of the way in such pleasant company. Fairfax spoke of stocks with such apparent knowledge that the colonel imagined him to be a gentleman of large property. It is not surprising that he was deceived, for the conman really understood the subject of which he spoke, having been for several years a clerk in a broker's counting room on Wall Street. The loss of his situation was occasioned by his abstraction of some securities, part of which he had disposed of before he was detected. He was, in consequence, tried and sentenced to three years' imprisonment. At the end of this period he was released, with no further taste for an honest life, and he had since allied himself to the class who thrive by preying upon the community.

This was the man whom Colonel Preston proposed to take as his companion on his otherwise lonely ride home.

CHAPTER XVIII

RIDING WITH A HIGHWAYMAN

"Get into the coach, Mr. Fairfax," said Colonel Preston.

"Thank you," said the conman, and he accepted the invitation.

"Now we are off," said the colonel, as he took the reins and touched the horse lightly with the whip.

"Is the road a pleasant one?" inquired Fairfax.

"The latter part is rather lonely. For a mile it runs through the woods; still, on a summer day, that is rather pleasant. In the evening, it is not so agreeable."

"No, I suppose not," said Fairfax rather absently.

Colonel Preston would have been startled could he have read the thoughts that were passing through the mind of his companion. Could he have known his sinister designs, he would scarcely have sat at his side, chatting so easily and indifferently.

"I will postpone my plan till we get to that part of the road he speaks of," thought Fairfax. "It would not do for me to be interrupted."

"I suppose it is quite safe traveling anywhere on the road," remarked the conman.

"Oh, yes," said Colonel Preston with a laugh. "Thieves and highway robbers do not pay us the compliment of visiting our neighborhood. They keep in the large cities or in places that will better reward their efforts."

"Precisely," said Fairfax. "I am glad to hear it, for I carry a considerable amount of money about me."

"So do I, today. This is the day for payment of mill dividends, and as I have occasion to use the money, I did not deposit it."

"Good," said Fairfax to himself. "That is what I wanted to find out."

Aloud he said, "Oh, well, there are two of us, so it would be a bold highwayman that would venture to attack us. Do you carry a pistol?"

"Not I," said Colonel Preston. "I don't like the idea of carrying firearms with me. They might go off by mistake. I was recently reading in a daily paper of a case where a man accidentally shot his son with the pistol he was in the habit of carrying with him."

"There is that disadvantage, to be sure," said Fairfax. "So, he has no pistol. He is quite in my power," he said to himself. "It's a good thing to know."

"By the way," he asked merely to keep up the conversation, "are you a family man, Colonel Preston?"

"Yes, sir. I have a wife and a son of fifteen."

"You have the advantage of me in that respect. I have always been devoted to business and have had no time for matrimony."

"Time enough yet, Mr. Fairfax."

"Oh, yes, I suppose so."

"If you are going to settle down in our neighborhood, I can introduce you to some of our marriageable young ladies," said Colonel Preston pleasantly.

"Thank you," said Fairfax in the same tone. "I may avail myself of your offer."

"Won't you take supper at my home this evening?" said the colonel hospitably. "I shall be glad to introduce Mrs. Preston. My son is at boarding school, so I shall not be able to let you see him."

"Have you but one child, then?"

"But one. His absence leaves us alone."

Godfrey's absence would have been lamented more by his father, had his character and disposition been different. But he was so arrogant and overbearing in his manners, and so selfish, that his father hoped that association with other boys would cure him in part of these objectionable traits. At home, he was so much indulged by his mother -- who could see no fault in him, as long as he did not oppose her -- that there was little chance of amendment.

So they rode on, conversing on various topics, but their conversation was not of sufficient importance for me to report. At length they entered on a portion of the road lined on either side by a natural forest. Fairfax looked about him.

"I suppose, Colonel Preston, these are the woods you referred to?"

"Yes, sir."

"How far do they extend?"

"About a mile."

They had traversed about half a mile, when Fairfax said, "If you don't object, Colonel Preston, I will step out a moment. There's a tree with a peculiar leaf. I would like to examine it more closely."

"Certainly, Mr. Fairfax," said the colonel, though he wondered what tree it could be, for he saw no tree of an unusual character.

The coach stopped and Fairfax jumped off. But he seemed to have forgotten the object of dismounting. Instead of examining the foliage of a tree, he stepped to the horse's head and seized him by the bridle.

"What are you going to do, Mr. Fairfax?" asked Colonel Preston in surprise.

By this time Fairfax had withdrawn a pistol from his inside pocket, and he deliberately pointed it at his companion.

A horse wearing a bridle

"Good heavens! Mr. Fairfax, what do you mean?"

"Colonel Preston," said the conman, "I want all the money you have about you. I know you have a considerable sum, for you have yourself acknowledged it."

"Why," exclaimed Colonel Preston, startled, "this is highway robbery."

"Precisely!" said Fairfax, bowing mockingly. "You have had the honor of riding with a highwayman. Will you be good enough to give me the money at once? I am in haste."

"Surely, this is a joke, Mr. Fairfax. I have heard of such practical jokes before. You are testing my courage. I am not in the least frightened. Jump in the coach again, and we will proceed."

"That's a very kind way of putting it," said Fairfax coolly, "but not correct. I am no counterfeit but am the genuine article. Fairfax is not my name. I won't tell you what it is, for it might be inconvenient."

No man can look with equanimity upon the prospect of losing money, and Colonel Preston may be excused for not wishing to part with his eight hundred dollars. But how could he escape? He had no pistol, and Fairfax held the horse's bridle in a strong grasp. If he could only deliberate with him till some carriage should come up, he might save his money. It seemed the only way, and he resolved to try it.

"Mr. Fairfax," he said, "if you are really what you represent, I hope you will consider the natural end of such a career. Turn, I entreat you, to a more honest course of life."

"That may come some time," said Fairfax, "but at present my necessities are too great. Oblige me by producing your wallet."

"I will give you one hundred dollars and keep the matter a secret from all. That will be better than to expose yourself to the penalty of the law."

"Colonel Preston, a hundred dollars will not satisfy me. You have eight hundred dollars with you, and I shall not leave this spot till it is transferred to my possession."

"If I refuse?"

"You will subject me to the unpleasant alternative of blowing your brains out," said the other coolly.

"You surely would not be guilty of such a crime, Mr. Fairfax?" said Colonel Preston with a shudder.

"I would rather not. I have no desire to take your life, but I must have that money. If you prefer to keep your money, you will compel me to the act. You'll gain nothing, for in that case I shall take both -- your life first and your money afterward."

"And this is the man with whom I dined and with whom, a few moments ago, I was conversing freely!" thought Colonel Preston.

The highwayman became impatient.

"Colonel Preston," he said abruptly, "produce that money instantly, or I will fire."

There was no alternative. With reluctant hand the colonel drew out his wallet and was about to hand it with its contents to the highwayman, when there was a sudden crash in the bushes behind

Fairfax. His pistol was dashed from his hand, and our young hero -- Andy Burke, with a resolute face -- stood with his gun leveled at him. Everything happened so quickly that both Colonel Preston and Fairfax were taken by surprise, and the latter, still retaining his hold upon the bridle, stared at the young hero who had so intrepidly come between him and his intended victim.

With an oath he stopped and was about to pick up the pistol, which had fallen from his hands, but he was arrested by the quick, decisive tones of Andy.

"Let that pistol alone! If you pick it up, I will shoot you on the spot."

CHAPTER XIX

BAFFLED A ROBBER

Fairfax paused at Andy's threat. He was only a boy, it is true, but he looked cool and resolute, and the gun, which was pointed at him, looked positively dangerous. But was he to be thwarted, in the very moment of his triumph, by a boy? He could not endure it.

"Young man," he said, "this is dangerous business for you. If you don't make yourself scarce, you won't be likely to return at all."

"I'll take the risk," said Andy coolly.

"Confound him! I thought he'd be frightened," said Fairfax to himself.

"I don't want to kill you," he said, with a further attempt to intimidate Andy.

"I don't mean to let you," said our hero quietly.

"You are no match for me."

"With a gun I am."

"I don't believe it is loaded."

"If you try to pick up that pistol, I'll convince you -- by the powers, I will," said Andy energetically.

"What is to prevent my taking away the gun from you?"

"Well," returned Andy quaintly, "you'll take the powder and ball first, I'm thinkin'."

Fairfax thought so, too, and that was one reason why he concluded not to try it.

It was certainly a provoking position for him.

There lay the pistol on the ground, just at his feet; yet, if he tried to pick it up, the boy would put a bullet through him. It was furthermore provoking to reflect that, had he not stopped to negotiate with Colonel Preston, he might have secured the money, which he so much desired, before Andy had come up. There was one other resource. He had tried bullying and without success. He would try cajoling and temptation.

"Look here, boy," he said, "I am a desperate man. I would as soon murder you as not."

"Thank you," said Andy. "But I'd rather not have it done."

"I don't want to hurt you, as I said before, but you mustn't interfere with me."

"Then you mustn't interfere with the colonel."

"I must have the money in his wallet."

"Must you? Maybe, I'll have something to say to that."

"He has eight hundred dollars with him."

"Did he tell you?"

"No matter; I know. If you won't interfere with me, I'll give you two hundred of it."

"Thank you for nothing, then," said Andy independently. "I'm only a poor Irish boy, but I ain't a thafe, and I never mane to be."

"Bravo, Andy!" said Colonel Preston, who had awaited with a little anxiety the result of the offer.

Fairfax stooped suddenly, but before he could get hold of the pistol, Andy struck him on the head with the gun-barrel, causing him to roll over while, in a quick and adroit movement, he himself got hold of the pistol before Fairfax had recovered from the crack on his head.

"Now," said Andy triumphantly, with the gun over his shoulder, and presenting the pistol, "lave here mighty quick, or I'll shoot ye."

"Give me back the pistol, then," said the discomfited ruffian.

"I guess not," said Andy.

"It's my property."

"I don't know that. Maybe you took it from some traveler."

"Give it to me, and I'll go off peaceably."

"I won't take no robber's word," said Andy. "Are you goin'?"

"Give me the pistol. Fire it off, if you like."

"That you may load it again. You don't catch a weasel asleep," answered Andy shrewdly. "I've a great mind to make you march into the village and give you up to the perlice."

This suggestion was by no means pleasant for the highwayman, particularly as he reflected that Andy had shown himself a resolute boy, and doubly armed as he now was, it was quite within his power to carry out his threat.

"Don't fire after me," he said.

"I never attack an inimy in the rare," said Andy, who always indulged in the brogue more than usual under exciting circumstances. I make this explanation, as the reader may have noticed a difference in his dialect at different times.

"We shall meet again, boy!" said Fairfax menacingly, turning at the distance of a few feet.

"Thank you, sir. You needn't thrubble yourself," said Andy, "I ain't anxious to mate you."

"When we do meet, you'll know it," said the other.

"Maybe I will. Go along wid ye!" said Andy, pointing the pistol at him.

"Don't shoot," said Fairfax hastily, and he quickened his pace to get out of the way of a dangerous companion.

Andy laughed as the highwayman disappeared in the distance.

"I thought he wouldn't wait long," he said.

"Andy," said Colonel Preston warmly, "you have behaved like a hero."

"I'm only an Irish boy," said Andy laughing. "Shure, they don't make heroes of such as I."

"I don't care whether you are Irish or Dutch. You are a hero for all that."

"Shure, sir, it's lucky I was 'round whin that spalpeen wanted to rob you."

"How did you happen to be out with a gun this afternoon?"

"I got my work all done, and Miss Grant said I might go out shootin' if I wanted. Shure, I didn't expect it 'ud been robbers I would be afther shootin'."

"You came up just in the nick of time. Weren't you afraid?"

"I didn't stop to think of that when I saw that big blackguard p'intin' his pistol at you. I thought I'd have a hand in it myself."

"Jump into the coach, Andy, and ride home with me."

"What, wid the gun?"

"To be sure. We won't leave the gun. That has done us too good a service already today."

"I've made something out of it, anyway," said Andy displaying the pistol, which was silver-mounted and altogether a very pretty weapon. "It's a regular beauty," he said with admiration.

"It will be better in your hands than in the real owner's," said Colonel Preston.

By this time Andy was in the chaise, rapidly nearing the village.

"If you hadn't come up just as you did, Andy, I should have been poorer by eight hundred dollars."

"That's a big pile of money," said Andy, who, as we know, was not in the habit of having large sums of money in his own possession.

"It is considerably more than I would like to lose," said Colonel Preston, to whom it was of less importance than to Andy.

"I wonder, will I ever have so much money?" thought Andy.

"Now, I'll tell you what I think is only right to do, Andy," pursued the colonel.

Andy listened attentively.

"I am going to make you a present of some money, as an acknowledgment of the service you have done me."

"I don't want anything, Colonel Preston," said Andy. "I didn't help you for the money."

"I know you didn't, my lad," said the colonel, "but I mean to give it to you all the same."

He took out his wallet, but Andy made one more remonstrance.

"I don't think I ought to take it, sir, thankin' you all the same."

"Then I will give you one hundred dollars for your mother. You can't refuse it for her."

Andy's eyes danced with delight. He knew how much good this money would do for his mother and how it would relieve her from the necessity of working so hard, as she was now compelled to do.

"Thank you, sir," he said. "It'll make my mother's heart glad and save her from the hard work."

"Here is the money, Andy," said the colonel, handing his young companion a roll of bills.

Again Andy poured out warm protestations of gratitude for the munificent gift, with which Colonel Preston was well pleased.

"I believe you are a good boy, Andy," he said. "It is a good sign when a boy thinks so much of his mother."

"I'd be ashamed not to, sir," said Andy.

They soon reached the village. Andy got down at the Misses Grant's gate and was soon astonishing the simple ladies by a narrative of his encounter with the highwayman.

"Do you think he'll come here?" asked Sophia in alarm. "If he should come when Andy was away -- "

"You could fire the gun yourself, Miss Sophia."

"I should be frightened to death."

"Then he couldn't kill you afterward."

"Just so," answered Sophia, a little bewildered.

"Were you shot, Andrew?" she asked a minute afterward.

"If I was, I didn't feel it," said Andy jocosely.

Andy's heroic achievement made him still more valued by the Misses Grant. They rejoiced in the handsome gift he had received from the colonel and readily gave him permission to carry it to his mother after supper.

CHAPTER XX

HOW THE NEWS WAS RECEIVED

It is always pleasant to carry good news, and Andy hastened with joyful feet to his mother's humble dwelling.

"Why, Andy, you're out of breath. What's happened?" asked Mrs. Burke.

"I was afraid of bein' robbed," said Andy.

"The robber wouldn't get much who would steal from you, Andy."

"I don't know that, mother. I ain't so poor as you think. Look there, now!"

Here he displayed the roll of bills. There were twenty five-dollar-bills, which made quite a thick roll.

"Where did you get so much, Andy?" asked his sister Mary.

"How much is it?" asked his mother.

"A hundred dollars," answered Andy proudly.

"A hundred dollars!" repeated his mother with apprehension. "Oh, Andy, I hope you haven't been stealing?"

"Did you ever know me to stale, mother?" said Andy.

"No, but I thought you might be tempted. Whose money is it?"

"It's yours, mother."

"Mine!" exclaimed Mrs. Burke in astonishment. "You're joking now, Andy."

"No, I'm not. It's yours."

"Where did it come from, then?"

"Colonel Preston sent it to you as a present."

"I am afraid you are not tellin' me the truth, Andy," said his mother doubtfully. "Why should he send me so much money?"

"Listen, and I'll tell you, mother, and you'll see it's the truth I've been tellin'."

Thereupon he told the story of his adventure with the highwayman and how he had saved Colonel Preston from being robbed.

His mother listened with pride, for though Andy spoke modestly, she could see that he had acted in a brave and manly way, and it made her proud of him.

"So the colonel," Andy concluded, "wanted to give me a hundred dollars, but I didn't like to take it myself. But when he said he would give it to you, I couldn't say anything ag'inst that. So here it is, mother, and I hope you'll spend some of it on yourself."

"I don't feel as if it belonged to me, Andy. It was you that he meant it for."

"Keep it, mother, and it'll do to use it when we nade it."

"I don't like to keep so much money in the house, Andy. We might be robbed."

"You can put part of it in the savings bank, mother."

This course was adopted. Andy himself carried eighty dollars and deposited it in a savings bank in Melville a few days afterward.

Meanwhile, at home Colonel Preston told the story of Andy's prowess.

But Mrs. Preston was prejudiced against Andy, and she listened coldly.

"It seems to me, Colonel Preston," she said, "you are making altogether too much of that Irish boy. He puts on enough airs to make one sick already."

"I never observed it, my dear," said the colonel mildly.

"Everyone else does. He thought himself on a level with our Godfrey."

"He is Godfrey's superior in some respects."

"Oh, well, if you are going to exalt him above your own flesh and blood, I won't stay and listen to you."

"You disturb yourself unnecessarily, my dear. I have no intention of adopting him in place of my son. But he has done me a great service this afternoon, and he displayed a coolness and courage very unusual in a boy of his age. If it were not for him, I should be eight hundred dollars poorer."

"Oh, well, you can give him fifty cents, and he will be well paid for his services, as you call them."

"Fifty cents!" repeated her husband.

"Well, a dollar, if you like."

"I have given him a hundred dollars."

"A hundred dollars!" almost screamed Mrs. Preston, who was a very mean woman. "Are you insane?"

"Not that I am aware of, my dear."

"It is perfectly preposterous to give such a sum to such a boy."

"I ought to say that I gave it to him for his mother. He was not willing to accept it for himself."

"That's a likely story," said Mrs. Preston incredulously. "He only wants to make a favorable impression upon you -- perhaps to get more out of you."

"You misjudge him, my dear."

"I know he is an artful, intriguing young rascal. You give him a hundred dollars, yet you refused to give Godfrey ten dollars last week."

"For a very good reason. He has a liberal allowance and must keep within it. He did not need the money he asked for."

"Yet you lavish a hundred dollars on this boy."

"I felt justified in doing so. Which was better: to give him that sum, or to lose eight hundred?"

"I don't like the boy, and I never shall. I suppose he will be strutting around, boasting of his great achievement. If he had a gun, it was nothing impressive."

"I suspect Godfrey would hardly have ventured upon it," said the colonel smiling.

"Oh, of course, Godfrey is vastly inferior to the Irish boy!" remarked Mrs. Preston ironically. "You admire the family so much that I suppose if I were taken away, you would marry his mother and establish her in my place."

"If you have any such apprehensions, my dear, your best course is to outlive her. That will effectually prevent my marrying her, and I pledge you my word that, while you are alive, I shall not think of eloping with her."

"It is very well to jest about it," said Mrs. Preston tossing her head.

"I am precisely of your opinion, my dear. As you observe, that is precisely what I am doing."

So the interview terminated. It was very provoking to Mrs. Preston that her husband should have given away a hundred dollars to Andy Burke's mother, but the thing was done and could not be undone. However, she wrote an account of the affair to Godfrey, who, she knew, would sympathize fully with her view of the case. Here are some extracts from her letter:

"Your father seems perfectly infatuated with that low Irish boy. Of course, I allude to Andy Burke. He has gone so far as to give him a hundred dollars. Yesterday, in riding home from Melville, with eight hundred dollars in his wallet, he says he was stopped by a highwayman who demanded his money or his life. Very singularly, Andy came up just in the nick of time with a gun, made a great show of interfering, and finally drove the man away, as your father reports. He is full of praise of Andy and, as I said, gave him a hundred dollars, when two or three would have been quite enough, even if the rescue had been real. But of this I have my doubts. It is very strange that the boy should have been on the spot just at the right time, still more strange that a full-grown man should have been frightened away by a boy of fifteen. In fact, I think it is what they call a 'put-up job.' I think the robber and Andy were confederates and that the whole thing was cut and dried, that the man should make the attack, and that Andy should appear and frighten him away, for the sake of a reward which I dare say the two have shared together. This is what I think about the matter. I haven't said so to your father, because he is so infatuated with the Irish boy that it would only make him angry, but I have no doubt that you will agree with me. [It may be said here that Godfrey eagerly adopted his mother's view and was equally provoked at his father's generosity to his young enemy.] Your father says he won't give you the ten dollars you asked for. He can lavish a hundred dollars on Andy, but he has no money to give his own son. But sooner or later that boy will be found out; sooner or later he will show himself in his true colors, and your father will be obliged to confess that he has been deceived. It puts me out of patience when I think of him.

"We shall expect you home on Friday afternoon of next week, as usual."

Andy was quite unconscious of the large space which he occupied in the thoughts of Mrs. Preston and Godfrey and of the extent to which he troubled them. He went on, trying to do his duty, and succeeding fully in satisfying the Misses Grant, who had come to feel a strong interest in his welfare.

Three weeks later, Sophia Grant, who had been to the village store on an errand, returned home looking greatly alarmed.

"What is the matter, Sophia?" asked her sister. "You look as if you had seen a ghost."

"Just so, Priscilla," she said. "No, I don't mean that, but we may all be ghosts in a short time."

"What do you mean?"

"Smallpox is in town!"

"Who's got it?"

"Colonel Preston, and his wife won't stay in the house. She is packing up to go off, and I expect the poor man'll die all by himself, unless somebody goes and takes care of him, and then it'll spread, and we'll all die of it."

This was certainly startling intelligence. Andy pitied the colonel, who had always treated him well. It occurred to him that his mother had passed through an attack of smallpox in her youth and could take care of the colonel without danger. He resolved to consult her about it at once.

CHAPTER XXI

A MODEL WIFE

Colonel Preston, returning from a trip to Boston -- in which, probably, he had been unconsciously exposed to the terrible disease referred to -- was taken sick, and his wife, wholly unsuspicious of her husband's malady, sent for the doctor.

The latter examined his patient and, on leaving the sick-chamber, beckoned Mrs. Preston to follow him.

"What is the matter with him, doctor?" asked Mrs. Preston. The physician looked grave.

"I regret to say, Mrs. Preston, that he has smallpox."

"Smallpox!" almost shrieked Mrs. Preston. "Oh! What will become of me?"

Dr. Townley was rather disgusted to find that her first thought was about herself and not about her stricken husband.

"It's contagious, isn't it, doctor?" she asked in great agitation.

"I am sorry to say that it is, madam."

"Do you think I will catch it?"

"I cannot take it upon myself to say."

And I was in the same room with him," wailed Mrs. Preston, "and never knew the awful danger! Oh, I wouldn't have smallpox for this world! If I didn't die, I should be all marked up for life."

"You haven't much beauty to spoil," thought the doctor, but this thought he prudently kept to himself.

"I must leave the house at once. I will go to my brother's house till he has recovered," said Mrs. Preston in agitation.

"What!" exclaimed the doctor in surprise, "and leave your husband alone!"

"I can't take care of him -- you must see that I can't," said Mrs. Preston fretfully. "I can't expose my life without doing him any good."

"I expose myself every time I visit him," said the doctor. "I never had smallpox. Have you been vaccinated?"

"Yes, I believe so -- I'm sure I don't know. But people sometimes get smallpox even after they have been vaccinated. I should be so frightened that I could do no good."

"Then," said the doctor gravely, "you have decided to leave your husband?"

"Yes, doctor, I must. It is my duty -- to my boy," answered Mrs. Preston, catching at this excuse with eagerness. "I must live for him, you know. Of course, if I could do any good, it would be different. But what would Godfrey do if both his father and mother should die?"

She looked up into his face, hoping that he would express approval of her intentions, but the doctor was too honest for this. In truth, he was disgusted with the woman's selfishness and would like to have said so, but this politeness forbade. At any rate, he was not going to be trapped into any approval of her selfish and cowardly determination.

"What do you wish to be done, Mrs. Preston?" he asked. "Of course, your husband must be taken care of."

"Hire a nurse, doctor. A nurse will do much more good than I could. She will know just what to do. Most of them have had smallpox. It is really much better for my husband that it should be so. Of course, you can pay high wages -- anything she asks," added Mrs. Preston, whose great fear made her, for once in her life, generous.

"I suppose that will be the best thing to do. You wish me, then, to hire a nurse?"

"Yes, doctor, if you will be so kind."

"When do you go away?"

"At once. I shall pack up my clothes immediately. On the whole, I think I will go to the town where Godfrey is at school and board there for the present. I must see him and prevent him from coming home."

"You will go into your husband's chamber and bid him goodbye?"

"No, I cannot think of it. It would only be useless exposure."

"What will he think?"

"Explain it to him, doctor. Tell him that I hope he will get well very soon and that I feel it my duty to go away now on Godfrey's account. I am sure he will see that it is my duty."

"I wonder what excuse she would have if she had no son for a pretext?" thought the doctor.

"Well," he said, "I will do as you request."

"See that he has the best of care. Get him two nurses, if you think best. Don't spare expense."

"What extraordinary generosity in Mrs. Preston," thought the physician.

He went back into the chamber of his patient.

"Doctor," said Colonel Preston, "you didn't tell me what was the matter with me. Am I seriously sick?"

"I am sorry to say that you are."

"Dangerously?"

"Not necessarily. You have smallpox."

"Have I?" said the patient thoughtfully.

It's an awkward thing to tell him that his wife is going to leave him," the doctor said to himself. "However, it must be done."

"Have you told my wife, doctor?"

"I just told her."

"What does she say?"

"She is very much startled and (now for it), thinks, under the circumstances, she ought not to run the risk of taking care of you on account of Godfrey."

"Perhaps she is right," said Colonel Preston slowly.

He was not surprised to hear it, but it gave him a pang, nevertheless.

"She wants me to engage a nurse for you."

"Yes, that will be necessary."

There was a pause.

"When is she going?" he asked, a little later.

"As soon as possible. She is going to board near the school where Godfrey is placed."

"Shall I see her?"

"She thinks it best not to risk coming into the chamber, lest she should carry the infection to Godfrey."

"I suppose that is only prudent," returned the sick man, but in his heart he wished that his wife had shown less prudence and a little more feeling for him.

"Have you thought of any nurse?" he asked.

"I have thought of the Widow Burke."

"She might not dare to come."

"She has had the disease. I know this from a few slight marks still left on her face. Of course, you would be willing to pay a generous price?"

"Any price," said Colonel Preston energetically. "It is a service which, I assure you, I shall not soon forget."

"I must see her at once, for your wife will leave directly."

"Pray, do so," said Colonel Preston. "Tell my wife," he said after a pause, "that I hope soon to have recovered, so that it may be safe for her to come back."

There was a subdued bitterness in his voice, which the doctor detected and did not wonder at. He gave the message, as requested.

"I am sure I hope so, Dr. Townley," said Mrs. Preston. "I shall be tortured with anxiety. I hope you will write me daily how my poor husband is getting along?"

"Perhaps the paper might carry the infection," said the doctor, testing the real extent of her solicitude.

"I didn't think of that," answered Mrs. Preston hastily. "On the whole, you needn't write, then. It might communicate the disease to Godfrey."

"She finds Godfrey very useful," the doctor thought.

"I will bear my anxiety as I can," she continued. "Have you thought of anyone for a nurse?"

"I have thought of Mrs. Burke."

"She is poor and will come if you offer her a good price. Try to get her."

"I think she will come. I must go at once, for your husband needs immediate attention."

"Get her to come at once, Dr. Townley! Oh, do! My husband may want something, and I can't go into the room. My duty to my dear, only son will not permit me. I hope Mr. Preston understands my motives in going away?"

"I presume he does," said the doctor rather equivocally.

"Tell him how great a sacrifice it is for me to leave his bedside. It is a terrible trial for me, but my duty to my son makes it imperative."

The doctor bowed.

He drove at once to the humble dwelling of Mrs. Burke.

His errand was briefly explained.

"Can you come?" he asked. "I am authorized to offer you ten dollars a week for the time you spend there."

"I would come in a minute, doctor, but what shall I do with Mary?"

"She shall stay at my house. I will gladly take charge of her."

"You are very kind, doctor. I wouldn't want to expose her, but I don't mind myself. I don't think I am in danger, for I've had smallpox already."

"Can you be ready in five minutes? Tell Mary to pack up her things and go to my house at once. We'll take good care of her."

In less than an hour Mrs. Burke was installed at the bedside of the sick man as his nurse. As she entered the house, Mrs. Preston left it, bound for the railway depot.

"I'm so glad you're here," she said, greeting the Widow Burke with unusual cordiality. "I am sure you will take the best care of my husband. I have told the doctor to pay you whatever you ask."

"I'll do my best, Mrs. Preston, but not for the money," answered Mrs. Burke. "Your husband shall get well, if good care can cure him."

"I've no doubt of it. But the carriage is here, and I must go. Tell my husband how sorry I am to leave him."

So Mrs. Preston went away, leaving a stranger to fulfill her own duties at the bedside of her husband.

Thus it happened that, when Andy came home, he found his mother already gone and his sister on the point of starting for the doctor's house. His idea had already been carried out.

CHAPTER XXII

COLONEL PRESTON'S RECOVERY

Four weeks later, we will introduce the reader into the bedchamber of Colonel Preston. His sickness had been severe. At times recovery was doubtful, but Mrs. Burke proved a careful and devoted nurse, intelligent and faithful enough to carry out the directions of the physician.

"How do you feel this morning, Colonel Preston?" asked the doctor, who had just entered the chamber.

"Better, doctor. I feel quite an appetite."

"You are looking better -- decidedly better. The disease has spent its force and retreated from the field."

"It is to you that the credit belongs, Dr. Townley."

"Only in part. The greater share belongs to your faithful nurse, Mrs. Burke."

"I shall not soon forget my obligations to her," said the sick man significantly.

"Now, Colonel Preston," said Mrs. Burke, "you are making too much of what little I have done."

"That is impossible, Mrs. Burke. It is to your good nursing and the doctor's skill that I owe my life, and I hardly know who to thank the most."

"To the doctor, sir. I only followed out his directions."

"At the expense of your own health. You show the effects of your long-continued care."

"It won't take long to pick up," said Mrs. Burke cheerfully.

"Is the danger of contagion over, doctor?" asked the patient.

"Quite so."

"Then, would it not be well to write to Mrs. Preston? Not that I mean to give up my good nurse just yet -- that is, if she is willing to stay."

"I will stay as long as you need me, sir."

"That is well, but Mrs. Preston may wish to return now that there's no further danger."

"I will write to her at once."

"Thank you."

The following letter was dispatched to Mrs. Preston:
MRS. PRESTON:

Dear Madam:

It gives me great pleasure to inform you that your husband is so far recovered that there is no danger now of infection. You can return with safety, and he will, doubtless, be glad to see you. He has been very ill -- indeed in danger of his life -- but thanks to the devotion of Mrs. Burke, who has proved an admirable nurse, he is now on the high road to recovery.

Yours respectfully,

John Townley

"I think that will bring her," said the doctor.

But he reckoned without his host.

The next day he received the following letter, on scented paper:

My dear Doctor Townley:

You cannot think how rejoiced I am to receive the tidings of my husband's convalescence. I have been so tortured with anxiety during the last four weeks! You cannot think how wretchedly anxious I have been. I could not have endured to stay away from his bedside but that my duty imperatively required it. I have lost flesh, and my anxiety has worn upon me. Now, how gladly will I resume my place at the bedside of my husband, restored by your skill. I am glad the nurse has proved faithful. It was a good chance for her, for she shall be well paid, and no doubt the money will be welcome.

But don't you think it might be more prudent for me to defer my return until next week? It will be safer, I think, and I owe it to my boy to be very careful. You know, the contagion may still exist. It is hard for me to remain longer away, when I would fain fly to the bedside of Mr. Preston, but I feel that it is best. Say to him, with my love, that he may expect me next week. Accept my thanks for your attention to him. I shall never forget it, and believe me to be, my dear doctor, your obliged,

Lucinda Preston

Dr. Townley threw down this letter with deep disgust.

"Was ever any woman more disgustingly selfish?" he exclaimed. "Her husband might have died, so far as she was concerned."

Of course, he had to show this letter to Colonel Preston.

The latter read it with a grave face, and the doctor thought he heard a sigh.

"My wife is very prudent," he said with a touch of bitterness in his voice.

"   She will be here next week," said the doctor, having nothing else to answer.

"I think she will run no risk then," said the sick man cynically.

But Mrs. Preston did not return in a week. It was a full week and a half before she arrived at her own house.

The doctor was just coming out of the front door.

"How is my husband?" she asked.

"Not far from well. He is still weak, of course."

"And are you sure," she said anxiously, "that there is no danger of infection?"

"Not the slightest, madam," said Dr. Townley coldly.

"I am so glad I can see him once more. You cannot imagine," she exclaimed, clasping her hands, "how much I have suffered in my suspense!"

The doctor remained cool and unmoved. He didn't feel that he could respond fittingly, being absolutely incredulous.

Mrs. Preston saw it and was nettled. She knew that she was a hypocrite, but she did not like to have the doctor, by his silence, imply his own conviction of it.

"Mine has been a hard position," she continued.

"Your husband has not had an easy time," said the doctor significantly.

"But he has had good care -- Mrs. Burke was a good nurse?"

"Admirable."

"She must be paid well."

"I offered her ten dollars a week."

"Humph!" said Mrs. Preston doubtfully, in whose eyes five dollars would have been generous compensation. "It has been a good chance for her."

"It is far from adequate," said the doctor disgusted. "Money cannot pay for such service as hers, not to speak of the risk she ran, for cases have been known of persons being twice attacked by the disease."

"You don't think my husband will have a relapse?" asked Mrs. Preston with fresh alarm.

"Not if he has the same care for a short time longer."

"He shall have it. She must stay. Of course her duties are lighter now, and six dollars a week for the remainder of the time will be enough -- don't you think so?"

"No, I don't," said the doctor bluntly, "and moreover, I am quite sure your husband will not consent to reducing the wages of one whose faithful care has saved his life."

"Oh, well, you know best," said Mrs. Preston slowly. "I am quite willing that she should be well paid."

Mrs. Preston went upstairs and entered her husband's chamber.

"Oh, my dear husband!" she exclaimed theatrically, hurrying across the room with affected emotion. "I am so glad to find you so much better!"

"I am glad to see you back, Lucinda," said Colonel Preston, but he spoke coldly and without the slightest affectation of sentimental joy. "I have passed through a good deal since you left me."

"And so have I!" exclaimed his wife. "Oh, how my heart has been rent with anxiety, as I thought of you lying sick, while duty kept me from your side."

"Is Godfrey well?" asked her husband, taking no notice of her last speech.

"Yes, poor boy! He sends his love and is so anxious to see you."

"Let him come next Friday afternoon," said the sick man, who doubted this statement yet wanted to believe it true.

"He shall. I will write to him at once."

So Mrs. Preston resumed her place in the house. But from that time on there was a something she could not understand in her husband's manner. He was graver than formerly, and sometimes she saw him watching her intently and, after a little, turn away with a sigh.

He had seen her in all her intense selfishness and want of feeling, and he could never again regard her as formerly, even though she tried hard at times, by a show of affection, to cover up her heartless neglect.

CHAPTER XXIII

MRS. BURKE HAS GOOD FORTUNE

Mrs. Burke remained a week longer to nurse Colonel Preston. At the end of this time Mr. Preston thought he was well enough to dispense with a nurse, and accordingly she prepared to take leave.

"I shall always remember your kind service, Mrs. Burke," said the colonel warmly.

"It was only my duty, sir," said the widow modestly.

"Not all would have done their duty so faithfully."

"I am glad to see you well again," said the widow.

"Not more than I am to get well, I assure you," said he. "Whenever you are in any trouble, come to me."

With these words, he placed in her hands an envelope, which, as she understood, contained the compensation for her services. She thanked him and took her departure.

Mrs. Burke acts as a dutiful nurse.

Mrs. Preston was curious to know how much her husband paid the nurse, and she asked the question.

"A hundred dollars," he replied.

"A hundred dollars!" she repeated, in a tone which implied disapproval. "I thought she agreed to come for ten dollars a week."

"So she did."

"She has not been here ten weeks -- only about six."

"That is true, but she has richly earned all I gave her."

"Ten dollars a week I consider very handsome remuneration to one in her position in life," said Mrs. Preston pointedly.

"Lucinda, but for her attention I probably should not have lived through this sickness. Do you think a hundred dollars so much to pay for your husband's life?"

"You exaggerate the value of her services," said his wife.

"Dr. Townley says the same thing that I do."

"You are both infatuated with that woman," said Mrs. Preston impatiently.

"We only do her justice."

"Oh, well, have it your own way. But I should have only paid her what I agreed to. It is a great windfall for her."

"She deserves it."

Mrs. Preston said no more at this time, for she found her husband too "infatuated," as she termed it, to agree with her. She did, however, open the subject to Godfrey when he came home, and he adopted her view of the case.

"She and her low son are trying to get all they can out of father," he said. "It's just like them."

"I wish I could make your father see it," said Mrs. Preston, "but he seems prepossessed in her favor."

"If he can give a hundred dollars to her, he can give me a little extra money. I'm going to ask him."

So he did the same evening.

"Will you give me ten dollars, father?" he asked.

"What for?"

"Oh, for various things. I need it."

"I give you an allowance of three dollars a week."

"I have a good many expenses."

"That will meet all your reasonable expenses. I was far from having as much money as that when I was of your age."

"I don't see why you won't give me the money," said Godfrey discontentedly.

"I don't think you need it."

"You are generous enough to others."

"To whom do you refer?"

"You give plenty of money to that Irish boy and his mother."

"They have both rendered me great services. The boy saved me from being robbed. The mother, in all probability, saved me from falling victim to smallpox. But that has nothing to do with your affairs. It is scarcely proper for a boy like you to criticise his father's way of disposing his money."

"I confess I think Godfrey is right in commenting upon your extraordinary generosity to the Burkes," observed Mrs. Preston.

"Lucinda," said her husband gravely, "when my own wife deserted my sick bed, leaving me to wrestle alone with a terrible and dangerous disease, I was fortunate enough to find in Mrs. Burke a devoted nurse. The money I have paid her is no adequate compensation, nor is it all that I intend to do for her."

There was a part of this speech that startled Mrs. Preston. Never before had her husband complained of her desertion of him in his sickness, and she hoped that he had been impressed by the excuse which she gave of saving herself for Godfrey. Now she saw that in this she had not been altogether successful, and she regretted having referred to Mrs. Burke and thus bringing this reproach upon herself. She felt it necessary to say something in extenuation.

"It was because I wanted to live for Godfrey," she said, with a flushed face. "Nothing but that would have taken me away from you at such a time. It was a great trial to me," she continued, putting up her handkerchief to eyes that were perfectly dry.

"We will say no more about it," said Colonel Preston gravely. "I shall not refer to it, unless you undervalue my obligations to Mrs. Burke."

Mrs. Preston thought it best not to reply, but on one thing that her husband had said, she later commented to Godfrey.

"Your father speaks of giving more money to Mrs. Burke. I suppose we shall not know anything about it if he does."

"Perhaps he will leave her some money in his will," said Godfrey.

"Very likely. If he does, there is such a thing as contesting a will -- that is, if he gives her very much."

Mrs. Preston was right. Her husband did intend to give his devoted nurse something in his will, but of that more later. There was one thing which he did at once, and that was to buy the cottage which Mrs. Burke occupied from the heir, a non-resident. Mrs. Burke didn't learn this until she went to pay her rent to the storekeeper, who had acted as agent for the owner.

"I have nothing to do with the house any longer, Mrs. Burke," he said.

"Then who shall I pay rent to?" said Mrs. Burke.

"To Colonel Preston, who has recently bought the house."

Mrs. Burke, therefore, called at the house of the colonel.

Mr. and Mrs. Preston were sitting together when the servant announced that she wished to speak to him.

"You seem to have a good deal of business with Mrs. Burke," said his wife in a very unpleasant tone.

"None that I care to conceal," he said smiling. "Show Mrs. Burke in here, Jane," he continued, addressing the servant.

"Good morning, Mrs. Burke," he said pleasantly.

"Good morning," said Mrs. Preston coldly.

"Good morning, sir. I'm glad to see you looking so much better."

"Oh, yes, I am feeling pretty well now."

"I didn't find out till just now, Colonel Preston, that you were my landlord."

Here Mrs. Preston pricked up her ears, for it was news to her also, as her husband had not mentioned his recent purchase.

"Yes, I thought I would buy the house, as it was on the market."

"I have come to pay my rent. I have been in the habit of paying fifteen dollars a quarter."

"I won't be a hard landlord," said Colonel Preston. "You are welcome to live in the house, if it suits you, free of all rent."

"This is too much kindness," said Mrs. Burke, quite overwhelmed by the unexpected generosity.

Mrs. Preston thought so, too, but she could not well say anything.

"There's been kindness on both sides, Mrs. Burke. Put away your money. I don't want it, but I have no doubt you will find use for it. Buy yourself a new dress."

"Thank you, Colonel Preston. You are very generous, and I am very grateful," said the widow.

"I have something to be grateful for also, Mrs. Burke. If you want any repairs, just let me know, and they shall be attended to."

"Thank you, sir, but the house is very comfortable."

She soon took her leave.

"When did you buy that house, Colonel Preston?" asked his wife.

"A month ago."

"You didn't say anything about it to me."

"Nor to anyone else, except those with whom I did the business."

Mrs. Preston would like to have said more, but she did not think it expedient, remembering what she had brought upon herself before.

CHAPTER XXIV

ANDY'S JOURNEY

Toward the first of April of the following year, Miss Sophia Grant caught a severe cold. It was not serious, indeed, but it was such as to make it prudent for her to remain indoors. This occasioned a little derangement of her sister's plans, for both sisters were in the habit of taking a journey to Boston around the first of April and the first of October. They did so partly for a change and partly because certain banks, in which they owned stock, declared dividends at these times, and they took the opportunity to collect these dividends. But this spring it seemed doubtful if they could go. Yet they wanted the money, or a part of it, at least.

"Send Andrew," suggested Miss Sophia, after her sister had stated the difficulty.

In general Miss Priscilla did not approve of Sophia's suggestions, but this struck her more favorably.

"I don't know but we might," she said slowly. "He is a boy to be trusted."

"Just so."

"And I think he is a smart boy."

"Indeed."

"He can take care of himself. You remember how he saved Colonel Preston from the robber?"

"Yes."

"Then, on the other hand, he has never been to Boston."

"He could ask."

"I don't suppose there would be any particular difficulty. I could give him all the necessary directions."

"Just so."

"I'll propose it to him."

So, after supper, as Andy was going out into the woodshed for an armful of wood, Miss Priscilla stopped him.

"Were you ever in Boston, Andy?" asked she.

"No, ma'am."

"I wish you had been."

"Why, ma'am?"

"Because I should like to send you there on some business."

"I'll go, ma'am," said Andy eagerly.

Like most boys of his age, no proposition could have been more agreeable.

"Do you think you could find your way there and around the city?"

"No fear of that, ma'am," said Andy confidently.

"We generally go ourselves, as you know, but my sister is sick, and I don't like to leave her."

"Of course not, ma'am," said Andy, quite approving any plan that opened the way for a journey to him.

"We own bank stock, and on the first of April they pay us dividends. Now, if we send you, do you think you can get to the bank, get the money, and bring it back safely?"

"I'll do it for you, ma'am," said Andy.

"Well, I'll think about it between now and next week. If we send you at all, you must start next Monday."

"I'll go any day, ma'am," said Andy. "Any day you name."

Miss Priscilla finally decided to send Andrew, but she cautioned him against saying anything about it except to his own family.

On Monday morning, just before the morning train was to start, Andrew appeared on the platform of the modest village depot with a small carpetbag in his hand, lent to him by the Misses Grant.

"Give me a ticket to Boston," said he to the station master.

Godfrey Preston, who was about to return to his boarding school, had just purchased a ticket and overheard this. He didn't much care to speak to Andy, but his curiosity overcame his pride.

"Are you going to Boston?" he asked.

"Yes," said Andy.

"What are you going for?"

"Important business."

"Has Miss Grant fired you?"

"She didn't say anything about it this morning. Why, do you want to take my place?"

"Do you think I'd stoop to be a hired boy?" said Godfrey haughtily.

"You wouldn't need to stoop," said Andy. "You ain't too tall."

Godfrey winced at this. He was not tall for his age, and he wanted to be. Andy had been growing faster than he and was now, though scarcely as old, quite two inches taller.

"It makes no difference about being tall," he rejoined. "I am a gentleman and don't have to work for a living like you do."

"What are you going to be when you grow up?"

"A lawyer."

"Then won't you work for money?"

"Of course."

"Then you'll be a hired man, and you'll work for a living."

"That's very different. When are you coming back?"

"When I've finished my business."

"How soon will that be?"

"I can't tell yet."

"Humph! I shouldn't wonder if you were running away."

"Don't you tell anybody," said Andy in a bantering tone.

"Where did you get the money to pay for your ticket?"

"What would you give to know?"

"You are impudent," said Godfrey, his cheek flushing.

"So are your questions," said Andy.

"I dare say you stole it."

"Look here, Godfrey Preston," said Andy, roused to indignation by this insinuation. "You'd better not say that again, if you know what's best for yourself."

He advanced a step with a threatening look, and Godfrey instinctively receded.

"That's what I get for speaking to my inferior," he said.

"That's not possible."

"What do you mean?"

"I don't know anybody that's inferior to you."

Godfrey turned on his heel wrathfully, muttering something about a "low beggar," which Andy, not hearing, did not resent.

The whistle of the locomotive was heard, and the cars came along.

With high anticipation of pleasure, Andy got aboard. He had before him a journey of close to a hundred miles, and he wished it had been longer. He had never been much of a traveler, and the scenes which were to greet his eyes were all novel. He had also heard a good deal of Boston, and he wanted to see it.

Besides the money which Miss Grant had given him to defray his expenses, he had with him ten dollars of his own. Since his mother had received the two donations from Colonel Preston she made Andy keep half his wages for his own use. These wages were now seven dollars a week, so he kept three and a half, and of this sum was able to save about half, or about two dollars a week. So he had a supply of money in his trunk, including his own ten dollars.

"Maybe I'll see something I want to buy in the city," he said to himself.

I don't mean to dwell upon the journey. There is nothing very exciting in a railway trip nowadays, even of a hundred miles, unless, indeed, the cars run off the track or over the embankment, and then it is altogether too exciting to be agreeable. For the sake of my young hero, though he is "only an Irish boy," I am glad to say that nothing of that sort took place. But in good time -- about the time when the clock on the Old South steeple indicated noon -- Andy's train drove into the Boston & Maine Railway depot, fronting on Haymarket Square.

"Ask how to get to Washington Street."

That was the first direction that Andy had received from Miss Priscilla, and that was what our hero did first.

The question was addressed to a very civil young man who politely gave Andy the necessary directions. So, in a short time, Andy reached Washington Street by way of Court Street.

The next thing was to inquire the way to the Merchants' Bank, the one in which the ladies owned the largest amount of stock.

"Where is the Merchants' Bank?" asked Andy of a boy, whose blacking-box denoted his occupation.

"I'll show you, mister," said the boy. "Come along."

His young guide, instead of taking him to the bank, took him to the side door of the courthouse and said, "Go in there."

It was a massive stone building, and Andy, not suspecting that he was being fooled, went in. Wandering at random, he found his way into a room where a trial was going on. That opened his eyes.

"He cheated me," thought Andy. "Maybe I'll get even with him."

He retraced his steps and again found himself in the street. His fraudulent young guide, with a grin on a face not overly clean, was awaiting his appearance.

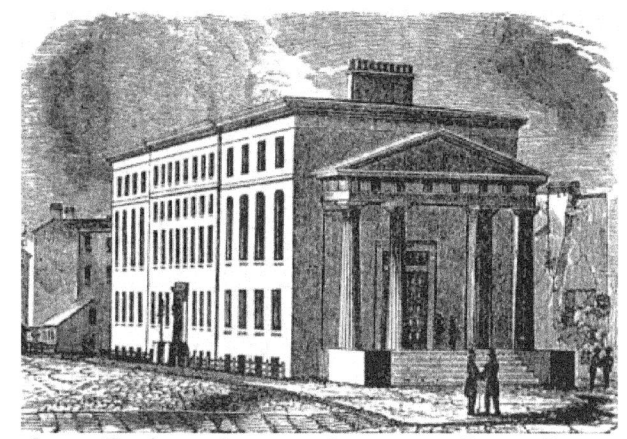
Andy walks into the courthouse on Court Street in Boston before realizing he's been tricked.

CHAPTER XXV

THE MERCHANT FROM PORTLAND

"Look here, young chap," said Andy, "what made you tell me that was the Merchants' Bank?"

"Isn't it?" asked the bootblack with a grin.

"It's the bank where you'll be wanted some time. Shouldn't wonder if they'd make a mistake and lock you up instead of your money."

"Have you got any money in the Merchants' Bank?" asked the other.

"I'm goin' to see if they won't give me some. If you hadn't cheated me, maybe I'd have invited you to dine with me at my hotel."

"Where are you stoppin'?" asked the street boy, not quite knowing how much of Andy's story to believe.

"At the most fashionable hotel."

"Parker's?"

"You're good at guessin'. Perhaps you'd like to dine there?"

"I don't know as they'd let me in," said the boy doubtfully, "but I'll show you where there's a nice eatin' house where they don't charge half so much."

"'Twouldn't be fashionable enough for me. I shall have to dine alone. See what comes of tryin' to fool your grandfather."

Andy went on, leaving the boy in doubt whether his jest had really lost him a lunch.

Andy didn't go to the Parker House, however. His expenses were to be paid by the Misses Grant, and he felt that it wouldn't be right to be extravagant at their expense.

"I shall come across an eatin' house presently," he said to himself.

Not far off he found one with the bill of fare and the prices exposed outside. Andy examined it and found that it was not an expensive place. He really felt hungry after his morning's ride and determined, before he attended to his business, to get lunch. He accordingly entered and seated himself at one of the tables. A waiter came up and awaited his commands.

"What'll you have?" he asked.

"Bring me a plate of roast beef and a cup of coffee," said Andy, "and be quick about it, for I haven't eaten anything for three weeks."

"Then I don't think one plate will be enough for you," said the waiter laughing.

"It'll do to begin on," said Andy.

The order was quickly filled, and Andy set to work energetically.

It is strange how we run across acquaintances when we least expect it. Andy had no idea that he knew anybody in the eating house and therefore didn't look around, feeling no special interest in the company. Yet there was one present who recognized him as soon as he entered and who watched him with strong interest. The interest was not friendly, however, as might be inferred from the scowl with which he surveyed him. This will not be a matter of surprise to the reader when I say that the observer was no other than Fairfax, whose attempt to rob Colonel Preston had been defeated by Andy.

He recognized the boy at once, both from his appearance and his voice, and deep feelings of resentment ran in his chest. To be foiled was disagreeable enough, but to be foiled by a boy was most humiliating, and he had vowed revenge if ever an opportunity occurred. For this reason he felt exultant when he saw his enemy walking into the eating house.

"I'll follow him," he said to himself, "and it'll be a shame if I don't get even with him for that trick he played on me."

But how did it happen that Andy did not recognize Fairfax?

For two reasons: first, because the conman was sitting behind him, and our hero faced the front of the room; next, had Andy seen him, it was doubtful he would have recognized a man whom he was far from expecting to see. This was because Fairfax was skilled in disguises, and he was no longer the black-whiskered individual who we formerly knew. From motives of prudence, he had shaved off his black hair and whiskers, and now appeared in a red wig and whiskers of the same hue. If any of my readers would like to know how effectual this disguise is, let them try it, and I will guarantee that they won't know themselves when they come to look at their likeness in the mirror.

After disposing of what he had ordered, Andy also ordered a plate of apple dumpling, which he ate with great satisfaction.

"I wouldn't mind eatin' here every day," he thought. "Maybe I'll be in business here some day myself, and then I'll come here and dine."

Fairfax was through with his lunch, but waited till Andy rose. He then rose and followed him to the desk, where both paid at the same time. He was careless of recognition, for he felt confident in his disguise.

"Now," thought Andy, "I must go to the bank."

But he didn't know where the bank was. So, when he got into the street, he asked a gentleman whom he met, "Sir, can you direct me to the Merchants' Bank?"

"It is on State Street," said the gentleman. "I am going past it, so if you will come along with me, I will show you."

"Thank you, sir," said our hero politely.

"Merchants' Bank!" said Fairfax to himself, beginning to feel interested. "I wonder what he's going there for? Perhaps I can raise a little money, besides having my revenge."

He had an added inducement now in following our hero.

When Andy went into the bank, Fairfax followed him. He was in the room when Andy received the dividends, and with sparkling eyes, he saw that it was a thick roll of bills, representing, no doubt, a considerable sum of money.

"That money must be mine," he said to himself. "It can't be the boy's. He must have been sent by some other person. The loss will get him into trouble. Very likely he will be considered a thief. That would just suit me."

Andy was careful, however. He put the money into a pocketbook, or, rather, wallet, with which he had been supplied by the Misses Grant, put it in his inside pocket, and then buttoned his coat up tight. He was determined not to lose anything by carelessness.

But this was not his last business visit. There was another bank on the same street where it was necessary for him to call and receive dividends. Again Fairfax followed him, and again he saw Andy receive a considerable sum of money.

"There's fat pickings here," thought Fairfax. "Now, I must manage, in some way, to relieve him of that money. There's altogether too much for a youngster like him. Shouldn't wonder if the money belonged to that man I tried to rob. If so, all the better."

In this conjecture, as we know, Fairfax was mistaken. However, it made comparatively little difference to him whose money it was, as long as there was a chance of his getting it into his possession. The fact was, that his finances were not in a very flourishing condition just at present. He could have done better to follow some honest and respectable business, and avoid all the dishonest shifts and infractions of law to which he was compelled to resort, but he had started wrong, and it was difficult to persuade him that, even now, it would be much better for him to amend his life and ways. In this state of affairs he thought it a great piece of good luck that he should have fallen in with a boy in charge of a large sum of money, whom, from his youth and inexperience, he would have less trouble in robbing than an older person.

Andy had already decided how he would spend the afternoon. He had heard a good deal about the Boston Museum, its large collection of curiosities, and the plays that were performed there. One of the most pleasant anticipations he had was to visit this place, the paradise of country people. Now that his business was concluded, he determined to go there at once. But first he must ask for directions.

Turning around, he saw Fairfax without recognizing him.

"Can you direct me to the Boston Museum?" he asked.

"Certainly, with pleasure," said Fairfax with alacrity. "In fact, I am going there myself. I suppose you are going to the afternoon performance?"

"Yes, sir."

"Have you ever been there?"

"No, but I have heard a good deal about it. I don't live in the city."

"Nor do I," said Fairfax. "I am a merchant of Portland, Maine. I have come to the city to buy my winter stock of goods. As I only come twice a year, I generally try to enjoy myself a little while I am here. Do you stay in the city overnight?"

"Yes," said Andy.

"So do I. Here is the Boston Museum."

They had reached the museum which, as some of my readers are aware, is situated on Tremont Street.

Andy visits the Boston Museum with Mr. Fairfax.

"We can go up these stairs," said Fairfax. "If you don't object, we will take seats together."

"I shall be glad to have company," said Andy politely.

Reserved seats adjoining were furnished, and the conman and his intended victim entered the museum.

CHAPTER XXVI

SPINNING THE WEB

There was a short interval before the play commenced. During this time Andy examined the large stock of curiosities which have been gathered from all parts of the world for the gratification of visitors. Fairfax kept at his side and spoke freely of all they saw. There was something about him which seemed to Andy strangely familiar. Was it in his features or in his voice? He could not tell. The red whig and whiskers misled him. Andy finally attributed it as a mere chance resemblance to someone whom he had met formerly, and he dismissed it from his mind.

At length the increasing crowds pouring into the lecture room reminded them that the play was about to begin.

"Shall we go in and take our seats?" said Fairfax.

Andy assented, and they were speedily in their seats.

I do not propose to speak of the play. It was a novelty to Andy to see a dramatic representation, and he thoroughly enjoyed it. Fairfax was more accustomed to such things, but pretended to be equally interested, feeling that in this way he could ingratiate himself better into Andy's confidence.

At last it was over, and they went out of the building.

"How did you like it?" asked Fairfax.

"Tiptop," said Andy promptly. "Don't you think so?"

"Capital," answered Fairfax, with simulated delight. "I am glad I had company. I don't enjoy anything half as well alone. By the way, where do you plan to pass the night?"

"At some hotel -- I don't know which."

"Suppose you go to the Adams House. I've got to stop overnight somewhere, and it might be pleasanter going in company."

"Where is the Adams House?"

"On Washington Street, not very far off -- ten or fifteen minutes' walk."

"If it's a good place, I'm willing."

"It is an excellent hotel and moderate in price. We might go up there now, get a room, and then spend the evening where we like."

"Very well," said Andy.

They soon reached the Adams House -- a neat, unpretending hotel -- and entered. They walked up to the desk, and Fairfax spoke to the clerk.

"Can you give us a room?"

"Certainly. Enter your names."

"Shall we room together?" asked Fairfax calmly.

Now Andy, though he had had no objection to going to the theater with his present companion, did not care to take a room with a stranger, of whom he knew nothing. He might be a very respectable man, but somehow, Andy did not know why, there was something in his manner which inspired a little repulsion. Besides, he remembered that he had considerable money with him, and that consideration alone rendered it imprudent for him to put himself in the power of a companion. So he said, a little awkwardly, "I think we'd better take separate rooms."

"Very well," said Fairfax, in a tone of indifference, though he really felt very much disappointed. "I thought it might have been a little more sociable to be together."

Andy did not take the hint, except so far as to say, "We can take rooms alongside of each other."

"I can give you adjoining rooms, if you desire," said the clerk.

Fairfax here entered his name in the hotel register as "Nathaniel Marvin, Portland, Maine," while Andy put down his real address. His companion's was, of course, fictitious. He did not venture to give the name of Fairfax, as that might be recognized by Andy as that of the highwayman, with whose plans he had interfered.

A servant was called, and they went up to their rooms, which, as the clerk had promised, were found to be adjoining. They were precisely alike.

"Very comfortable, Mr. Burke," said Fairfax, in a tone of apparent satisfaction. "I think we shall have a comfortable night."

"I guess so," said Andy.

"Are you going to stay here now?"

"No, I'm going to wash my face and then take a walk around. I want to see something of the city."

"I think I'll lie down awhile; I feel tired. Perhaps we shall meet later. If not, I shall see you in the morning."

"All right," said Andy.

In a few minutes he went out.

CHAPTER XXVII

THE DROP GAME

Fairfax had a motive in remaining behind. He wanted to see if there was any way for him to get into Andy's room during the night so that he might rob him in his sleep. To his great satisfaction, he found that there was a door between the two rooms, for the accommodation of persons in the same party, who wished to be in adjoining apartments. It was, however, locked, but Fairfax was prepared for such an emergency. He took a bunch of keys from his pocket and tried them, one after another, in the lock. There was one that very nearly fit. For this again, Fairfax was prepared. He took from the same pocket a file and began patiently to file away the key till it should fit. He tried it several times before he found that it fit. At last success crowned his efforts. The door opened.

His eyes danced with exultation as he saw this.

"I might as well be in the same room," he said to himself. "Now, you young rascal, I shall take your money and be revenged upon you at the same time."

He carefully locked the door and then, feeling that he had done all that was necessary to do at present, went downstairs and took supper. Andy was out and did not see him.

Meanwhile, our young hero was out seeing the sights. He walked up Washington Street and at Boylston Street turned and reached Tremont Street, when he saw the Common before him. It looked pleasant, and Andy crossed the street and entered. He walked wherever fancy led and then, after a while, found himself in a comparatively secluded part of the city. Here he met with an adventure, which I must describe.

Rather a shabby-looking individual in front of him suddenly stooped and picked up a wallet, which appeared to be well filled with money. He looked up, and met Andy's eyes fixed upon it. This was what he wanted.

"Here's a wallet," he said. "Somebody must have dropped it."

Andy was interested.

"It seems to have considerable money in it," said the finder.

"Open it, and see," said Andy.

"I haven't time. I have got to leave the city by the next train. I mean, I haven't time to advertise it, and get the reward which the owner will be sure to offer. Are you going to stay in the city long?"

"I'm going out tomorrow."

"I must go. I wish I knew what to do."

He seemed to be plunged into anxious thought.

"I'll tell you what I'll do," he said, as if a bright idea had suddenly struck him. "You take the wallet and advertise it. If the owner is found, he will give you a reward. If not, the whole will belong to you."

"All right," said Andy. "Hand it over."

"Of course," said the other, "I shall expect something myself, as I was the one to find it."

"I'll give you half."

"But I shall be out of the city. I'll tell you what, give me ten dollars, and I'll make it over to you."

"That's rather steep," said Andy.

"Heft it. There must be a lot of money inside."

"I'm afraid the reward might be less than ten dollars," said Andy.

"Well, I'm in a great hurry -- give me five."

It is possible that Andy, who was not acquainted with the "drop game," might have agreed to this, but a policeman came into sight, and the shabby individual scuttled away without further ceremony leaving Andy a little surprised, with the wallet in his hand.

"What's he in such a hurry for?" thought our hero.

He opened the wallet, and a light flashed upon him, as he perceived that there was no money inside, but was stuffed with rolls of paper.

"He wanted to swindle me," thought Andy. "It's lucky I didn't pay him five dollars. Anyway, I'll keep it. The wallet is worth something."

He put it in his pocket, without taking the trouble to remove the contents.

CHAPTER XXVIII

THE GUEST OF TWO HOTELS

Andy wandered about till nine o'clock, determined to see as much of the city as possible in the limited time which he had at his disposal, but at last he became tired and returned to the hotel. Fairfax was seated in the reading room. He looked up as Andy entered.

"Have you been looking around the city?" he asked.

"Yes," said Andy. "I wanted to take advantage of my time here."

"I suppose, as this is your first visit, you see a good deal that is new?"

"It's all new," said Andy. "I feel tired, walking around so much."

"No doubt. Are you going to bed now?"

"I guess I'll turn in."

"I shan't go up quite yet. I have been staying here quietly, and I don't feel tired. I shall go up in the course of an hour or two."

"Good night, then," said Andy.

"Good night. I hope you'll sleep soundly," said Fairfax, who was certainly entirely sincere in this wish, as the success of his plans depended on the soundness of our hero's repose.

Andy went upstairs, and lighted the gas in his bedroom. He noticed the door connecting with the next room and tried it, but he found it to be locked.

"That's all right," said Andy. "Nobody can get in that way."

He locked the principal door and bolted it also, which seemed to make him perfectly secure.

"Now," thought he after undressing, "where shall I put the money?"

This was an important question, as he had between five hundred and a thousand dollars belonging to the Misses Grant, of which it was his duty to take even more care than if it belonged to himself.

"I guess I'll put it under the bolster," he reflected, "covering it up with the sheet. Nobody can get in, that I can see, but it is best to be careful."

In emptying his pockets, he came across the wallet, with its sham contents, of which mention has already been made.

"I'll leave that in my pocket," he said to himself with a smile. "I'm not afraid of losing that. By the powers, it wouldn't be much of a prize to the man that took it; I'm sure of that."

He laid his clothes on a chair in the middle of the room and jumped into bed, where he soon sank into a deep sleep.

Meanwhile, Fairfax remained below in the reading room. He was not at all sleepy, as he had told Andy, and his mind was full of the scheme of robbery, which appeared so promising. He was glad Andy had retired so early, as he would be asleep sooner, and this would make things favorable for his entering his young companion's chamber. After he had secured the "plunder" -- to adopt a Western phrase -- it was his intention to come downstairs and leave the hotel and not return, for as soon as Andy should discover his loss, the door between the two rooms would, naturally, point to him as the thief.

He didn't go up to his room till half-past ten. This was an hour and a half later than Andy retired and would give him a chance to be fast asleep.

"He must be asleep now," he thought.

On reaching the corridor, on which both of the chambers were situated, he stood a moment before Andy's door and listened. It was not often that our young hero was guilty of snoring, but tonight he was weary and had begun to indulge in this nocturnal disturbance. The sounds which he heard were very satisfactory to Fairfax.

"The boy's fast asleep," he muttered. "I'll go into his room and make quick work of it. Fairfax, you're in luck, for once. Fortune has taken a turn."

Softly he opened the door of his own room and entered. He lit the gas, and then, going to the door of communication between the two rooms, he listened again. There was no cessation of the sounds which he had heard from the outside. He determined to make the attempt at once. Taking the proper key from his pocket, he fitted it into the lock and, turning it, the door opened, and he stepped into the adjoining apartment. It was dark, for Andy had extinguished the gas before going to bed, but the gas from his own room made it sufficiently light for his purpose. He at once caught sight of Andy's clothes lying on the chair where he had placed them. He glanced cautiously at our hero, as he lay extended upon the bed with one arm flung out, but he saw no reason for alarm. Quickly he glided to the chair with noiseless step (he had removed his boots, by way of precaution), and thrust his hand into the pocket of the coat. It came in contact with the false wallet, which seemed bulky and full of money. Fairfax never doubted that it was the right one, and he quickly thrust it into his own pocket. Just then Andy moved a little in bed, and Fairfax retreated, hastily, through the door, closing it after him.

"Now, the sooner I get out of this hotel, the better!" he thought. "The boy may wake and discover his loss. It isn't likely, but it may happen. At any rate it's much better to be on the safe side."

He did not stop to examine the prize which he had secured. He had no doubt whatsoever that it contained the money he was after. To stop to count it might involve him in peril. He, therefore, put on his boots and glided out of the chamber and downstairs.

To the clerk who was at the desk he said, as he surrendered his key, "How late do you keep open? Till after midnight?"

"Certainly," was the reply.

"All right. I may be out till late."

He left the key and went out into the street. He hailed a passing car on Tremont Street and rode for some distance. On Court Street he got on board a Charlestown car, and in half an hour he found himself in the city known everywhere by the granite shaft that commemorates the battle of Bunker Hill. He made his way to a hotel where he took a room, entering here under the name of James Simmons, Portsmouth, New Hampshire. Anxious to examine his prize, he desired to be shown at once to a chamber. He followed the servant who conducted him with impatient steps. The stolen money was burning in his pocket. He wanted to know how much he had and was more than half resolved to take an early train the next morning for the West, where he thought he should be secure from discovery.

"Is there anything wanted, sir?" asked the servant, lingering at the door.

"No, no," said Fairfax impatiently. "It's all right."

"Might be a little more polite," muttered the snubbed servant, as he went downstairs.

"Now for it!" exclaimed Fairfax exultingly. "Now, let me see how much I have got."

He drew the wallet from his pocket and opened it. His heart gave a quick thump, and he turned ashy pale, as his glance rested upon the worthless roll of brown paper with which it had been stuffed.

"Curse the boy!" he cried, in fierce and bitter disappointment. "He has fooled me, after all! Why didn't I stop long enough to open the wallet before I came away? Blind, stupid fool that I was! I am as badly off as before -- nay, worse, for I have exposed myself to suspicion, and I haven't got a penny to show for it."

I will not dwell upon his bitter self-reproaches and, above all, the intense mortification he felt at having been so completely fooled by a boy, whom he had despised as verdant and inexperienced in the ways of the world -- to think that success had been in his grasp, and he had missed it after all, was certainly disagreeable enough. It occurred to him that he might go back to the Adams House even now and repair his blunder. It was not likely that Andy was awake yet. He was very weary, and boys of his age were likely, unless disturbed, to sleep through the night. He might retrieve his error, and no one would be the wiser.

"I'll do it," he said at length.

A hotel in Boston

He went downstairs and left the hotel without the knowledge of the clerk. Jumping into the horsecars, he returned to Boston and entered the Adams House about half-past twelve o'clock. He claimed his key at the desk and went upstairs to his room. He had scarcely lit the gas, however, when a knock was heard at the door. Opening it unsuspiciously, he turned pale, as he recognized the clerk, in company with an officer of the law.

"What's wanted?" he faltered.

"You are wanted," was the brief reply.

"What for?" he gasped.

"You are charged with entering the adjoining room and stealing a wallet from the boy who sleeps there."

"It's a lie!" he said, but his tone was nervous.

"You must submit to a search," said the officer.

"Do you mean to insult me?" demanded Fairfax, assuming an air of outraged virtue.

"Not at all. I am only giving you a chance to clear yourself from suspicion."

"I am a respectable merchant from Portland. I was never so insulted in my life," said Fairfax.

"If the charge proves groundless, I will make you an ample apology," said the officer.

Fairfax was compelled to submit to the search. He cursed his stupidity in not throwing away the worthless wallet, but this he had neglected to do, and, of course, it was very significant evidence against him. Not only was this found, but so was the variety of keys already referred to.

"You carry a great many keys," said the officer.

"It isn't a crime to carry keys, is it?" demanded Fairfax sullenly.

"Not if no improper use is made of them. I suspect that one of them will open the door into the next chamber."

The keys were tried, and one did open the door. As the light flashed into the room, Andy got up.

"Come here, young man," said the officer. "Can you identify that wallet?"

"I can," said Andy.

"Is it yours?"

"When I went to bed, it was in the pocket of my coat, lying on that chair."

"It is certainly a wonderful wallet. I have just found it in that gentleman's pocket."

Fairfax's eyes were bent malignantly upon Andy. A light flashed upon him. Now, he recognized him.

"I know you," he said. "You are the man that stopped Colonel Preston and tried to rob him."

"You lie, curse you!" exclaimed Fairfax, springing forward and trying to throw himself upon Andy. But he was not quick enough. The officer had interposed and seized him by the collar.

"Not so fast, Mr. Marvin, or whatever your name is. We don't allow any such games as that. Sit down till I want you."

The baffled conman was jerked into a chair, from which he continued to eye Andy savagely.

"What's that affair you were talking about, young man?" asked the officer.

Andy briefly related his adventure with Fairfax on a former occasion.

"I'll trouble you to come with me, Mr. Marvin, or Fairfax," said the officer. "There's another hotel where lodgings are provided for such as you."

Resistance was useless, and the detected thief, though his name was registered at two hotels, was compelled to occupy a less agreeable room at the stationhouse. How he was detected will be explained in the next chapter.

CHAPTER XXIX

A STARTLING EVENT

Sometimes, the mere presence of a person in the room is sufficient to interrupt even sound repose. At all events, whether it was the entrance of Fairfax, acting in some mysterious way upon Andy, or the light that streamed into the room, his slumber was disturbed, and his eyes opened just as the conman was retiring with his supposed booty.

Our hero did not immediately take in the situation. He was naturally a little bewildered, being just aroused from sleep, but in a short time the real state of the case dawned upon him.

"By the powers!" he said to himself, "it's that man that went to the museum with me! He saw my money, and he came in for it! I'll get up and see."

Quietly and noiselessly he got out of bed and, going to the chair, felt in his pockets, and so he discovered the loss of the stuffed wallet.

Andy wanted to laugh, but forbore, lest the sound should be heard in the next room.

"It's a good joke on the dirty thafe!" said Andy to himself. "He's welcome to all the money he's got -- it won't carry him far, I'm thinkin'."

Prudence suggested another thought. When Fairfax found out the worthlessness of his booty, would he not come back and search for the real treasure?

"If he does, I'll fight him," thought Andy.

Still, he knew the conflict would be unequal, since the other was considerably his superior in strength. However, Andy determined that, come what might, he would defend his trust, "or perish in the attempt." But, while he was coming to this determination, he heard the door of the adjoining chamber open softly, and then he could hear steps along the corridor. Evidently, the thief had not found out the actual character of his booty but was going off under the impression that it was valuable.

"Maybe he'll come back," thought Andy. "I guess I'd better go down and give notice at the desk. Then, if he comes back, he'll get into hot water."

He hastily dressed himself and, locking his door, went downstairs. First, however, he removed the money from under his pillow and put it into his pocket. He found the clerk at the desk.

"Has the man that came in with me gone out?" asked Andy.

"Mr. Marvin?"

"Yes."

"He went out about five minutes ago."

"Did he say anything about coming back?"

"He said it would be late when he returned. He asked me if we kept open after twelve. Did you want to find him?"

"I should like to have the police find him," said Andy.

"How is that?" asked the clerk surprised.

"He has robbed me."

"Did you leave your door unlocked?"

"No, but there was a door between our rooms. He opened it, and stole a wallet from the pocket of my coat."

"While you were asleep?"

"Yes, but I awoke just in time to see him go through the door."

"How much money was there in it?"

"That's the joke of it," said Andy laughing. "There was no money at all, only some folds of paper. He got hold of the wrong wallet."

Thereupon, he told the story of the "drop game," of which he came near being a victim and what a useful turn the bogus treasure had done him.

"There's the right wallet," he said in conclusion. "I wish you would take care of it for me till tomorrow. The money isn't mine, and I don't want to run any more risk with it."

"I'll lock it up in the safe for you," said the clerk. "Is there much?"

"Several hundred dollars."

"You were very fortunate in escaping as you did," said the clerk.

"True," said Andy. "He may come back when he finds out how he has been fooled."

"If he does, I'll call a policeman. We'll make short work with him."

The reader has already heard how Fairfax (or Marvin) did return, and how he met with a reception he had not calculated upon. Andy was informed in the morning that it would be necessary for him to appear as a witness against him in order to secure his conviction. This he did the next day, but the judge delayed sentence when he was informed that the accused was charged with a more serious offense, that of stopping a traveler on the highway. His trial on this count had to come before a higher court, and he was remanded in prison till his case was called from the calendar. Andy was informed that he would be summoned as a witness in that case also, as well as Colonel Preston, and answered that he would be ready when called upon.

We will so far anticipate events as to say that the testimony of Andy and the colonel was considered conclusive by the court, and, on the strength of it, Mr. Fairfax, alias Marvin, was sentenced to several years' imprisonment of hard labor.

Andy met with no further adventures in his present visit but had the satisfaction of delivering the money he had been sent to collect to Miss Priscilla Grant.

Now, advancing our story some three months, we come to an afternoon when Miss Sophia Grant, returning from a walk -- with visible marks of excitement -- rushed, breathless and panting, into her sister's presence.

"What's the matter, Sophia?" asked Priscilla.

"Such an awful thing!" she gasped.

"What is it?"

"You won't believe it."

"Tell me at once what it is!"

"It seems so sudden!"

"Good heavens! Sophia, why do you tantalize me so?"

"Just so!" gasped Sophia.

"If you don't tell me, I'll shake you!"

"Colonel Preston's dead -- dropped dead in the store ten minutes ago. I was there, and I saw him."

This startling intelligence was only too true. Suddenly, without an instant's warning, the colonel had been summoned from life -- succumbing to a stroke. This event, of course, made a great sensation in the village, but it is of most interest to us as it affects the fortunes of our young hero.

CHAPTER XXX

COLONEL PRESTON'S WILL

Mrs. Preston was a cold woman and was far from being a devoted wife. She was too selfish for that supreme love which some women bestow upon their husbands. Still, when Colonel Preston's lifeless form was brought into the house, she did experience a violent shock. To have the companion of nearly twenty years so unexpectedly taken away might well touch the most callous, and so, for a few minutes, Mrs. Preston forgot herself and thought of her husband.

But this was not for long. The thought of her own selfish interests came back, and in the midst of her apparent grief the question forced itself upon her consideration, "Did my husband make a will?"

Of course, she did not give utterance to this query. She knew what was expected of her, and she was prudent enough to keep up appearances before the neighbors, who poured into the house to offer their sympathy. She received them with her cambric handkerchief pressed to her eyes, from which, by dint of effort, she succeeded in squeezing a few formal tears, and, while her bosom appeared to heave with emotion, she was mentally calculating how much Colonel Preston had probably left.

"Shan't I stay with you, my dear Mrs. Preston?" said worthy Mrs. Cameron, in a tone full of warm interest and sympathy.

"Thank you," said Mrs. Preston in a low voice. "You are very kind, but I would rather be left alone."

"But it must be so sad for you to be alone in your sorrow," said her neighbor.

"No. I can bear sorrow better alone," said the newly made widow. "Perhaps I am peculiar, but I would prefer it."

"If you really wish it," said the other, reluctantly.

"Yes, I wish it. Thank you for your kind offer, but I know my own feelings, and the presence of others would only increase my pain."

This was what she said to others who made the same offer. It did not excite great surprise, for Mrs. Preston had never leaned upon anyone for sympathy, nor was she ready with her sympathy when others were in trouble. She was self-poised and self-contained and, in fact, for this reason was not popular with her neighbors. Still, in her distress they were ready to forget all this and extend the same cordial sympathy which they would have done in other cases. There was but one person whose company she did crave at this time and this was her son, Godfrey. So, when Alfred Turner offered to go call for him the next morning, she accepted his offer with thanks.

At last she was left alone. The servant had gone to bed, and there was no one but herself and her dead husband in the lower part of the house. She no longer sat with her handkerchief pressed before her eyes. Her face wore its usual look of calm composure. She was busily thinking, not of her husband's fate, but of her own future.

"Did he leave a will? And, if so, how much did he leave me?" she thought.

If there was a will, it was probably in the house, and Mrs. Preston determined to find it if possible.

"Of course, all ought to come to me and Godfrey," she soliloquized. "I don't think it is right to leave money to charitable institutions as long as a wife and child are living. Fortunately, my husband had no brothers or sisters, or perhaps he would have divided the property. If there is no will, I shall have my thirds and shall have the control of Godfrey's property till he comes of age. I think I will go to Boston to live. My friend, Mrs. Boynton, has a very pleasant house on Worcester Street. I should like to settle down somewhere near her. I don't know how much Mr. Preston was worth, but I am sure we shall have enough for that. I always wanted to live in the city. This village is intolerably stupid, and so are the people. I shall be glad to get away."

Could the good women, whose kind hearts had prompted them to proffer their sympathy, have heard these words they would not have been likely to obtrude any more on the hard, cold woman who held them in such low estimation.

Mrs. Preston took the lamp in her hand and began to explore her husband's desk. She had often thought of doing so, but, as his death was not supposed to be so near, she had not thought that there was any immediate cause of doing so. Besides, it had almost been her belief that he had made no will. Now she began to open drawers and untie parcels of papers, but it was some time before she came to what she sought. At length, however, her diligence was rewarded. In the middle of a pile of papers, she found one labeled on the outside: MY WILL.

Her heart beat as she opened it, and, though there was no need -- for it was now past ten o'clock, and there was not likely to be a caller at that late hour -- she looked cautiously about her and even peered out of the window into the darkness, but she could find no one whose observation she might fear.

I am not about to recite at length the items in the will, which covered an entire page. It is enough to quote two items, which Mrs. Preston read with anger and dissatisfaction. They were as follows:

"Item.—To my young friend, Andy Burke, son of the Widow Burke, of this village, in consideration of a valuable service rendered to me on one occasion and as a mark of my regard and interest, I give and bequeath the sum of five thousand dollars; and to his mother, as a token of gratitude for her faithful nursing when I was dangerously sick with smallpox, I give and bequeath, free of all encumbrance, the cottage in which she at present resides.

"Item.—To the town, I give five thousand dollars, the interest to be annually appropriated to the purchase of books for a public library, for the benefit of all the citizens, provided the town will provide some suitable place in which to keep them."

All the balance of the property was left to his wife and son, in equal proportions, his wife to be the guardian of Godfrey till he should have attained a certain age. As Colonel Preston was well known to be rich, this seemed to be an adequate provision, but Mrs. Preston did not look upon it in that light. On the contrary, she was deeply incensed at the two legacies of which mention has been made above.

"Was there ever anything more absurd than to waste five thousand dollars and a house upon that Irish boy and his mother?" she said to herself. "I don't suppose it was so much my husband's fault. That artful woman got around him, and wheedled him into it. I know now why she was so willing to come here and take care of him when he was sick. She wanted to wheedle him into leaving money to her low-lived boy. She is an artful and designing tease, and I should like to tell her so to her face."

The cold and usually impassible woman was deeply excited. Her selfish nature made her grudge any of her husband's estate to others, except, indeed, to Godfrey, who was the only person she cared for. As she thought over the unjust disposition -- as she regarded it -- which her husband had made of his property, a red spot glowed in her usually pale cheek.

Then it was another grievance that money should have been left to the town.

"What claim had the town on my husband," she thought, "that he should give it five thousand dollars? In doing it, he was robbing Godfrey and me. It was wrong. He had no right to do it. What do I care for these people? They are a set of common farmers and mechanics, with whom I condescend to associate because I have no one else here to speak to, except the minister's and the doctor's family. Soon I shall be in the city, and then I don't care if I never set eyes on any of them again. In Boston I can find suitable society."

The more Mrs. Preston thought of it, the more she felt aggravated by the thought that so large a share of her husband's property was to go to others. She fixed her eyes thoughtfully on the document which she held in her hand, and a strong temptation came to her.

"If this should disappear," she said to herself, "the money would be all mine and Godfrey's, and no one would be the wiser. That Irish boy and his mother would stay where they belonged, and my Godfrey would have his own. Why should I not burn it? It would only be just."

Deluding herself by this false view, she persuaded herself that it was right to suppress the will. With a steady hand she held it to the flame of the lamp and watched it as it was slowly consumed. Then, gathering up the fragments, she threw them away.

"It is all ours now," she whispered triumphantly, as she prepared to go to bed. "It was lucky I found the will."

CHAPTER XXXI

MRS. PRESTON'S INTENTIONS

Godfrey returned home on the day after his father's death. He had never witnessed death before, and it frightened him, for the time, into propriety. He exhibited none of the stormy and impetuous grief which a warm-hearted and affectionate boy would have been likely to exhibit. It was not in his nature.

When he and his mother were left alone, he showed his resemblance to her by asking, "Do you know how much property father left?"

"I don't know. He never told me about his affairs as he ought. I think he must have left near a hundred thousand dollars."

Godfrey's eyes sparkled.

"That's a pile of money," he said. "It goes to me, doesn't it?"

"To us," said Mrs. Preston.

"A woman doesn't need so much money as a man," said Godfrey selfishly.

"You are not a man yet," said his mother dryly. "Your father may have left a will. In that case, he may have left a part of his property to others."

"Do you think he has?" inquired Godfrey in alarm.

"I don't think any will will be found," said his mother quietly. "He never spoke to me of making one."

"Of course not. That wouldn't be fair, would it?"

"It is fitting that the property should all go to us."

"When shall I get mine?"

"When you are twenty-one."

"That's a long time to wait," grumbled Godfrey.

"You are only a boy yet. I shall probably be your guardian."

"I hope you'll give me a larger allowance than father did."

"I will."

"Must I go back to boarding school? I don't want to."

"If I go to Boston to live, as I think I shall, I will take you with me, and you can go to school there."

"That'll be jolly," said Godfrey, his eyes sparkling with anticipation. "I've got tired of this miserable town."

"So have I," said his mother. "We shall have more privileges in Boston."

"I can go to the theater as often as I please there, can't I?"

"We will see about that."

"How soon shall we move to the city?"

"As soon as business will allow. I must settle up your father's affairs here."

"Can't I go beforehand?"

"Would you leave me alone?" asked his mother, with a little touch of wounded affection, for she did feel attached to her son. He was the only one, indeed, for whom she felt any affection.

"You won't miss me, mother. It'll be awfully stupid here, and you know you'll be coming to the city as soon as you get through with the business."

Mrs. Preston was disappointed, but she should not have been surprised. Her only son reflected her own selfishness.

"It would not look well for you to go to the theater just at the present," she said.

"Why not?"

"So soon after your father's death."

Godfrey said nothing, but he looked discontented. It was early to think of amusement, while his father lay yet unburied in the next room. He left the room, whistling. He could not gainsay his mother's objections, but he thought it hard luck.

A funeral in a country village is a public occasion. Friends and neighbors are expected to be present without invitation. Among those who assembled at the house were Mrs. Burke and Andy. They felt truly sorry for the death of Colonel Preston, who had been a friend to both. Mrs. Preston saw them enter, and, notwithstanding the solemnity of the occasion, the thought intruded, "They're after the legacy, but they will be disappointed. I've taken good care of that."

Godfrey saw them, also, and his thought was a characteristic one, "What business has that Irish boy at my father's funeral? He ought to know better than to poke himself in where he is not wanted."

Even Godfrey, however, had the decency to let this thought remain unspoken. The services proceeded, and among those who followed on foot in the funeral procession were Andy and his mother. It never occurred to them that they were intruding. They wanted to show respect for the memory of one who had been a friend to them.

On the day after the funeral Squire Tisdale called at the house, invited by Mrs. Preston. The squire had a smattering of law and often acted as executor in settling estates.

"I invited you to come here, Squire Tisdale," said Mrs. Preston, "to speak about my affairs. Of course, it is very trying to me to think of business so soon after the death of my dear husband" -- here she pressed her handkerchief to her tearless eyes -- "but I feel it to be my duty to myself and my boy."

"Of course," said the squire soothingly. "We can't give way to our feelings, however much we want to."

"That is my feeling," said Mrs. Preston, whose manner was wonderfully cool and collected, considering the grief which she desired to have it thought she experienced for her husband.

"Did Colonel Preston leave a will?" asked the squire.

"I don't think he did. He never mentioned making one to me. Did you ever hear of his making any?"

"I can't say that I ever did. I suppose it will be best to search."

"Won't it be more proper for you to make the search, Squire Tisdale?" said the widow. "I am an interested party."

"Suppose we search together. You can tell me where your husband kept his private papers."

"Certainly. He kept them in his desk. I locked it as soon as he died, but here is the key. If there is a will, it is probably there."

"Very probably. We shall soon ascertain, then."

Squire Tisdale took the key, and Mrs. Preston led the way to her late husband's desk. A momentary fear seized her.

"What if there was an earlier will, or two copies of the last?" she thought. "I ought to have made sure by looking over the other papers."

But it was too late now. Besides, it seemed very improbable that there should be another will. Had there been an earlier one, it would, doubtless, have been destroyed on the drafting of the one she had found. She reassured herself, therefore, and awaited, with tranquility, the result of the search.

The search was careful and thorough. Mrs. Preston desired that it should be so. Knowing the wrong she had done to Andy and his mother, as well as the town, she was unnecessarily anxious to appear perfectly fair, and assured Squire Tisdale that, had there been a will, its provisions should have been carried out to the letter.

"There is no will here," said the squire after a careful search.

"I did not expect you would find one," said the widow, "but it was necessary to make sure."

"Is there any other place where your husband kept papers?"

"We will look in the drawers and trunks," said Mrs. Preston, "but I don't think any will be found."

None was found.

"Can I do anything more for you, Mrs. Preston?" asked the squire.

"I should like your advice, Squire Tisdale. I am not used to business, and I would like the aid of your experience."

"Willingly," said the squire, who felt flattered.

"As my husband left no will, I suppose the estate goes to my son and myself?"

"Undoubtedly."

"How ought I to proceed?"

"You should apply for letters of administration, which will enable you to settle up the property."

"Will you help me to take the necessary steps?"

"Certainly."

"I should like to settle the estate as rapidly as possible, as I intend to move to Boston."

"Indeed? We shall be sorry to lose you. Can you not content yourself here?"

"Everything will remind me of my poor husband," said Mrs. Preston, with another application of the handkerchief to her still tearless eyes.

Squire Tisdale was impressed with the idea that she had more feeling than he had thought.

"I didn't think of that," he said sympathetically. "No doubt you are right."

Mrs. Preston lost no time in applying for letters of administration.

"As soon as I get them," she said to herself, "I will lose no time in ejecting that Irishwoman from the house my husband bought for her. I'll make her pay rent, too, for the time she has been in it."

CHAPTER XXXII

MRS. PRESTON'S REVENGE

Andy Burke was passing the house of Mrs. Preston, within a month after Colonel Preston's death, when Godfrey, who had not gone back to boarding school, showed himself at the front door.

"Come here!" said Godfrey in an imperious tone.

Andy turned his head and paused.

"Who are you talking to?" he asked.

"To you, to be sure."

"What's wanted?"

"My mother wants to see you."

"All right. I'll come in."

" You can go around to the back door," said Godfrey, who seemed to find pleasure in making himself disagreeable.

"I know I can, but I don't mean to," said Andy, walking up to the front entrance where Godfrey was standing.

"The back door is good enough for you," said the other offensively.

"I shouldn't mind going to it if you hadn't asked me," said Andy. "Just move away, will you?"

Godfrey did not stir.

"Very well," said Andy turning. "Tell your mother you would not let me in."

"Come in, if you want to," said Godfrey, at length moving aside.

"I don't care much about it. I only came to oblige your mother."

"Maybe you won't like what she has to say," said Godfrey with a disagreeable smile.

"I'll soon know," said Andy.

He entered the house, and Godfrey called upstairs, "Mother, the Burke boy is here."

"I'll be down directly," was the answer. "He can sit down."

Andy sat down on a chair in the hall, not receiving an invitation to enter the sitting room, and waited for Mrs. Preston to appear. He wondered a little what she wanted with him, but thought it likely that she had some errand or service in which she wished to employ him. He did not know the extent of her dislike for him and his mother.

After a while Mrs. Preston came downstairs. She was dressed in black, but showed no other mark of sorrow for the loss of her husband. Indeed, she was looking in better health than usual.

"You can come into the sitting room," she said coldly.

Andy followed her, and so did Godfrey, who felt a malicious pleasure in hearing what he knew beforehand his mother intended to say.

"I believe your name is Andrew?" she commenced.

"Yes, ma'am."

"Your mother occupies a house belonging to my late husband."

"Yes, ma'am," answered Andy, who now began to guess at the object of the interview.

"I find, by examining my husband's papers, that she has paid no rent for the last six months."

"That's true," said Andy. "She offered to pay it, but Colonel Preston told her he didn't want any rent from her. He said she could have it for nothing."

"That's a likely story," said Godfrey with a sneer.

"It's a true story," said Andy, in a firm voice, steadily eying his young antagonist.

"This may be true, or it may not be true," said Mrs. Preston coldly. "If true, I suppose my husband gave your mother a paper of some kind, agreeing to let her have the house rent-free."

"She hasn't got any paper," said Andy.

"I thought not," said Godfrey, sneering. "You forgot to write her one."

"Be quiet, Godfrey," said his mother. "I prefer to manage this matter myself. Then, your mother has no paper to show in proof of what you assert?"

"No, ma'am. The colonel didn't think it was necessary. He just told my mother, when she first came with the rent, that she needn't trouble herself to come again on that errand. He said that she had nursed him when he was sick with smallpox, and he'd never forget it, and that he'd bought the house expressly for her."

"I am aware that your mother nursed my husband in his sickness," said Mrs. Preston coldly. "I also know that my husband paid her very handsomely for her services."

"That's true, ma'am," said Andy. "He was a fine, generous man, the colonel was, and I'll always say it."

"There really seems no reason why, in addition to this compensation, your mother should receive a present of her rent. How much rent did she pay before my husband bought the house?"

"Fifteen dollars a quarter."

"Then she has not paid rent for six months. I find she owes my husband's estate thirty dollars."

"Colonel Preston told her she wasn't to pay it."

"How do I know that?"

"My mother says it, and she wouldn't tell a lie," said Andy indignantly.

"I have nothing to say as to that," said Mrs. Preston. "I am now managing the estate, and the question rests with me. I decide that your mother has been sufficiently paid for her services, and I shall claim rent for the last six months."

Andy was silent for a moment. Then he spoke, "It may be so, Mrs. Preston. I'll speak to the doctor, and I'll do as he says."

"I don't know what the doctor has to do with the matter," said Mrs. Preston haughtily.

"He wants to get an excuse for not paying," said Godfrey with a sneer.

"Mind your business," said Andy, excusably provoked.

"Do you hear that, mother?" said Godfrey. "Are you going to let that beggar insult me before your very face?"

"You have spoken very improperly to my son," said Mrs. Preston.

"He spoke very improperly to me at first," said Andy sturdily.

"You do not appear to understand the respect due to me," said Mrs. Preston with emphasis.

"If I've treated you disrespectfully, I'm sorry," said Andy, "but Godfrey mustn't insult me and call me names."

"We have had enough of this," said Mrs. Preston. "I have only to repeat that your mother is indebted to me for six months' rent -- thirty dollars -- which I desire she will pay as soon as possible. One thing more: I must request her to find another home, as I have other plans for the house she occupies."

"You're not goin' to turn her out of her house, surely?" said Andy in some dismay.

"It is not her house," said Mrs. Preston, though it occurred to her that it might have been if she had not suppressed the will. But, of course, Andy knew nothing of this, nor did he suspect anything, since neither he nor his mother had the faintest idea of being remembered in Colonel Preston's will, kind though he had been to them both in his life.

"I know it isn't," said Andy; "but she's got used to it. I don't know any other place we can get."

"That is your concern," said Mrs. Preston. "I have no doubt you can get in somewhere. As I said, the house is mine, and I have other views for it."

"Can't we stay till the end of the quarter, ma'am?"

"No. I wish to finish my business here as soon as possible, and then I shall go to Boston."

"How long can we stay, then?"

"Till the first of the month."

"That's only three days."

"It is long enough to find another place. That is all I have to say," and Mrs. Preston turned to go.

Andy rose and followed her without a word. He saw that it would be of no use to appeal for more time. Her tone was so firm and determined that, evidently, there was no moving her.

"What will we do?" thought Andy, as he walked slowly and silently along the road.

He felt the need of consulting somebody older and more experienced than himself. Just in the nick of time he met Dr. Townley, in whose friendship he felt confidence.

"Can you stop a minute, Dr. Townley?" he said. "I want to speak to you about something."

"I can spare two minutes, if you like, Andy," said the doctor smiling.

Andy explained the case.

"It is quite true," said the doctor. "Colonel Preston intended your mother to pay no rent -- he told me so himself -- but as your mother has no written proof, I suppose you will have to pay it. Shall I lend you the money?"

"No need, doctor. We've got money enough for that. But we must move out in three days. Where shall we go?"

"I'll tell you. I own the small house occupied by Grant Melton. He sets out for the West tomorrow with his family. I'll rent it to your mother for the same rent she's been paying."

"Thank you," said Andy gratefully. "It's better than the house we've been living in. It's a good change."

"Perhaps you won't like me for a landlord so well as Mrs. Preston," said the doctor smiling.

"I'll risk it," said Andy.

Two days afterward the transfer was made. Mrs. Preston was disappointed, and Godfrey still more so, to find their malice had done the Widow Burke no harm.

By advice of the doctor, Andy deferred paying the thirty dollars claimed as rent, availing himself of the twelve months allowed for the payment of debts due the estate of one deceased.

"If it was anybody else, I'd pay at once," said Andy, "but Mrs. Preston has treated us so meanly that I don't mean to hurry."

The delay made Mrs. Preston angry, but she was advised that it was quite legal.

CHAPTER XXXIII

ANDY LOSES HIS JOB

Andy and his mother moved into Dr. Townley's cottage. It was rather an improvement upon the house in which they had lived hitherto, except for a great difference: for the one they had no rent to pay, but for the other they paid fifteen dollars rent. Dr. Townley would gladly have charged nothing, but he was a comparatively poor man and could not afford to be as generous as his heart would have dictated. He had a fair income, being skillful and in good practice, but he had a son in college, and his expenses were a considerable drain upon his father's purse. Still, with the money saved and Andy's weekly earnings, the Burkes were able to live very comfortably and still pay the rent. But a real misfortune was in store for Andy.

Miss Sophia Grant was taken sick with lung fever. The sickness lasted for some weeks and left her considerably debilitated.

"What do you think of Sophia, Dr. Townley?" asked Priscilla anxiously. "She remains weak, and she has a bad cough. I am feeling alarmed about her."

"I'll tell you what I think, Miss Priscilla," said the doctor, "though I am sorry to do it. The fact is, the air here is altogether too bracing for your sister. She will have to go to some inland town, where the east winds are not felt."

"Then I must go, too," said Miss Priscilla. "We have lived together from girlhood, and we cannot be separated."

"I supposed you would be unwilling to leave her, so I am afraid we must make up our minds to lose you both."

"Do you think, doctor, that Sophia will, by and by, be strong enough to return here?"

"I am afraid not. The effects of lung fever are always felt for a long time. She will improve, no doubt, but a return to this harsh air would, I fear, bring back her old trouble."

"I asked because I wanted to know whether it would be best to keep this place. After what you have told me, I shall try to sell it."

"I am truly sorry, Miss Priscilla."

"So am I, Dr. Townley. I don't expect any place will seem so much like home as this."

Have you any particular place that you can think of going to?"

"Yes. I have a niece married in a small town near Syracuse, New York. They don't have east winds there. I'll get Priscilla -- she's named after me -- to hunt up a cottage that we can live in, and we'll move right out there. I suppose we'd better go soon?"

"Better go at once. Weak lungs must be humored."

"Then I'll write to Priscilla to get me a boarding house, and we'll start next week."

There was one person whom this removal was likely to affect seriously, and this was our young hero.

"I hope Andy'll be able to get a job," said Priscilla, after she had communicated the doctor's orders to her sister.

"Just so, Priscilla. He's a good boy."

"I will give him a good recommendation."

"Does he know it?"

"No. I will call him in and tell him, so that he can be looking out for another position."

"Just so."

Andy answered the call of Miss Priscilla. He had been sawing wood, and there was sawdust in his sleeves.

"How long have you been with us, Andy?" asked his mistress.

"Over a year, ma'am."

"I wish I could keep you for a year to come."

"Can't you?" asked Andy, startled.

"No, Andy."

"What's the matter, Miss Priscilla? Have I done anything wrong?"

"No, Andy. We are both of us quite satisfied with you."

"You haven't lost any money, ma'am, have you? I'll work for less, if you can't afford to pay as much as you've been paying."

"Thank you, Andy, but it isn't that. My sister's lungs are weak, and Dr. Townley has ordered her to move to a less exposed place. We are going to move away from the town."

"I'm sorry," said Andy, and he was, for reasons other than because he was about to lose a good job.

"We shall miss you, Andy."

"Just so," chimed in Miss Sophia with a cough.

"You see how weak my sister's lungs are. It's on her account we are going."

"Shan't you come back again, ma'am?"

148

"No, Andy. The doctor says it will never be safe for us to do so. I hope you will get a good job."

"I hope so, ma'am, but you needn't think of that."

"We are prepared to give you a good recommendation. We feel perfectly satisfied with you in every way."

"Just so," said Sophia.

"Thank you, ma'am, and you, too, Miss Sophia. I've tried to do my duty faithfully by you."

"And you have, Andy."

"How soon do you go, ma'am?"

"Next week, if we can get away. The doctor says we can't get away soon enough. So you had better be looking around to see if you can get a job somewhere."

"I will, ma'am, but I'll stay with you till the last day. You'll need me to pack up for you."

"Yes, we shall. Tomorrow I'll write you the recommendation."

"Thank you, ma'am."

Andy did not sleep as much as usual that night. His wages were the main support of his mother and sister, and he could think of no other place in the village where he was likely to be employed. He had a little money saved up, but he didn't like the idea of spending it. Besides, it would not last long.

"I wish Dr. Townley wanted to hire a boy," thought Andy. "I'd rather work for the doctor than for anybody else in the village. He's a nice man, and he cares just as much for poor folks as he does for rich folks. I am sure he likes me better than he does Godfrey Preston."

But Dr. Townley already had a boy, whom he did not like to let go. Nor could he have afforded to pay Andy as high wages as he had received from the Misses Grant. There really seemed to be no vacant place in the village for our young hero to fill, and, of course, this troubled him.

Next week the Misses Grant left the village. They gave Andy a present of an old-fashioned silver watch, about the size and shape of a turnip. Andy was glad to get it, old-fashioned as it was, and he thanked them warmly.

The day afterward he was walking slowly along the village street when he came upon Godfrey Preston strutting along with an air of importance. He and his mother had moved to Boston, but they were visiting the town on a little business.

"Hello, there!" said Godfrey halting.

149

"Hello!" said Andy.

"You've lost your job, haven't you?" asked Godfrey with a sneer.

"Yes."

"How are you going to live?"

"By eating, I expect," answered Andy shortly.

"If you can get anything to eat, you mean?"

"We got enough so far."

"Perhaps you won't have, for long. You may have to go to the poorhouse."

"When I do, I shall find you there."

"What do you mean?" demanded Godfrey angrily.

"I mean I shan't go there till you do."

"You're proud for a beggar."

"I'm more of a gentleman than you are."

"I'd thrash you, only I won't demean myself by doing it."

"That's lucky, or you might get thrashed yourself."

"You're only an Irish boy."

"I'm proud of that all the same. You won't find me going back on my country."

Godfrey walked away. Somehow, he could never get the better of Andy.

"I hope I'll see you begging in rags, some day," he thought to himself.

But boys like Andy are not often reduced to such a point.

CHAPTER XXXIV

THE WILL AT LAST

The next three months passed very unsatisfactorily for Andy. In a small country town like that in which he lived there was little opportunity for a boy, however industrious, to earn money. The farmers generally had sons of their own or were already provided with assistants, and there was no manufacturing establishment in the village to furnish employment to those who didn't like agriculture. Andy had some idea of learning the carpenter trade, as there was a carpenter who was willing to take an apprentice, but unfortunately he was unwilling to pay any wages for the first year -- only boarding the apprentice -- and our hero felt, for his mother's sake, that it would not do to make such an engagement.

When the three months were over, the stock of money which Andy and his mother had saved up was almost gone. In fact, he had not enough left to pay the next quarter's rent to Dr. Townley.

Things were in this unsatisfactory state when something happened that had a material effect upon Andy's fortunes and, as my readers will be glad to know, for their improvement.

To explain what it was, I must go back to a period shortly before Colonel's Preston's death. One day he met the doctor in the street and stopped to speak to him.

"Dr. Townley," he said, "I have a favor to ask of you."

"I shall be very glad to serve you, Colonel Preston," said the doctor.

Thereupon Colonel Preston drew from his inside pocket a sealed envelope of large size.

"I want you to take charge of this for me," he said.

"Certainly," said the doctor in some surprise.

"Please read what I have written upon the envelope."

The doctor, his attention called to the envelope, read, inscribed in large, distinct characters:

Not to be opened till six months after my death.

"I see you want an explanation," said the colonel. "Here it is -- the paper contained in this envelope is an important one. I won't tell you what it is. When you come to open it, it will explain itself."

"But, colonel, you are likely to live as long as I. In that case, I can't follow your directions."

"Of course, we can't tell the duration of our lives. Still, I think you will outlive me. If not, I shall reclaim the paper. Meanwhile, I shall be glad to have you take charge of it for me."

"Of course I will. It is a slight favor to ask."

"It may prove important. By the way, there is no need of telling anyone, unless, perchance, your wife. I don't want to force you to keep anything secret from her. Mrs. Townley, I know, may be depended upon."

"I think she may. Well, Colonel Preston, set your mind at rest. I will take care of the paper."

When Colonel Preston died not long afterward, the doctor naturally thought of the paper, and, as no will was left, it occurred to him that this might be a will, but in that case he couldn't understand why he should have been enjoined to keep it six months before opening it. On the whole, he concluded that it was not a will.

Seated at the supper table, about this time, Mrs. Townley said, suddenly, "Henry, how long is it since Colonel Preston died?"

"Let me see," said the doctor thoughtfully. "It is -- yes, it is six months tomorrow."

"Then it is time for you to open that envelope he gave into your charge."

"So it is. My dear, your feminine curiosity inspired that thought," said the doctor smiling.

"Perhaps you are right. I admit that I am a little inquisitive in the matter."

"I am glad you mentioned it. I have so much on my mind that I should have let the day pass, and I should be sorry not to fulfill to the letter the promise I made to my friend."

"Have you any suspicion as to the nature of the document?"

"I thought it might be a will, but, if so, I can't understand why a delay of six months should have been interposed."

"Colonel Preston may have had his reasons. Possibly he did not fully trust his wife's attention to his requests."

"It may be so. I am afraid his married life was not altogether harmonious. Mrs. Preston always struck me as a very selfish woman."

"No doubt of that. She evidently regarded herself as superior to the rest of us."

"In that respect Godfrey is like her. He is a self-conceited, disagreeable young jackanapes. I wouldn't give much for his chances of honorable distinction in life. I'll tell you of a boy who will, in my opinion, beat him in the race of life."

"Who is that?"

"Andy Burke."

"Andy is a good boy, but I am afraid the family is doing poorly now."

"So I fear. The, fact is, there doesn't appear to be much opening for a lad like Andy in this village."

"I hear that Mr. Graves, the storekeeper, who is getting old, wants to get a boy or young man with a small capital to take an interest in his business and, eventually, succeed him."

"That would be a good chance for Andy, if he had the small capital, but he probably hasn't ten dollars in the world."

"That's a pity."

"If I were a capitalist, I wouldn't mind starting him myself, but as you, my dear, are my most precious property and are not readily convertible into cash, I don't quite see my way to do anything to assist him."

"I didn't think of you, Henry. Country doctors are not likely to get rich. But I thought Colonel Preston, who seemed to take an interest in the boy, might do something for him."

"If he had lived, he might have done so -- probably he would. But Mrs. Preston and Godfrey hate the Burkes like poison, for no good reason that I know of, and there is no chance of help from that quarter."

"I should think not."

The next day, Dr. Townley, immediately after breakfast, drew the envelope already referred to from among his private papers and, breaking the seal, opened it.

To his surprise and excitement, he discovered that the inclosure was the last will and testament of his deceased friend. Accompanying it was the following note:

My Dear Friend, Dr. Townley:

This is the duplicate of a will executed recently and expresses my well-considered wishes as to the disposition of my property. The original will may have been found and executed before you open this envelope. In that case, of course, this shall be of no value, and you can destroy it. But I am aware that valuable papers are liable to loss or injury, and, therefore, I deem it prudent to place this duplicate in your possession, that, if the other be lost, you may see it carried into execution. I have named you my executor and am sure, out of regard to me, you will accept the trust and fulfill it to the best of your ability.

I have always felt the utmost confidence in your friendship, and this will account for my troubling you on the present occasion.

Your friend,

Anthony Preston

From this letter Dr. Townley turned to the perusal of the will. The contents filled him with equal surprise and pleasure.

"Five thousand dollars to Andy Burke!" he repeated. "That is capital! It will start the boy in life, and with his good habits it will give him a sure income by and by. With half of it he can buy an interest in Graves' store, and the balance will, if well invested, give him a handsome addition to his income. Then there's the bequest for the town library -- a capital idea, that is! It will do a great deal to make the town attractive, and it will be a powerful agency for refining and educating the people."

Just then Mrs. Townley, who knew what her husband was about, came into the room.

"Well, Henry," she said, "is the paper important?"

"I should say it is. It is Colonel Preston's last will and testament."

"Is it possible? How does he leave his property?"

"He leaves five thousand dollars for a town library."

"Does he remember Andy Burke?"

"He leaves him five thousand dollars, and he gives his mother the house they used to live in."

"That's splendid! But what will Mrs. Preston say?"

"Well, that remains to be seen," said the doctor laughing.

CHAPTER XXXV

MRS. PRESTON IS

UNPLEASANTLY SURPRISED

Dr. Townley thought it best to consult with the town authorities as to the course to be pursued, since, as it appeared, the will concerned the town. It was decided that the doctor and Mr. Graves, who was the Chairman of the Selectmen, should go to Boston the next day and inform Mrs. Preston of the discovery of the will. Until after this interview it was deemed best not to mention the matter to Andy or his mother.

Mrs. Preston was established in a showy house at the South End. At last she was living as she desired to do. She went to the theater and the opera and was thinking whether she could afford to set up a carriage. Godfrey she had placed at a private school, and she was anxious to have him prepare for admission to Harvard College, but in this hope she seemed destined to be disappointed. Godfrey wanted to see life and enjoy himself and had no intention of submitting to the drudgery of hard study.

"Godfrey," said his mother one morning, "I have received a letter from your teacher complaining that you don't work."

"I'm not going to work myself to death," answered Godfrey.

"I don't expect you to hurt yourself with work, but I want you to go to college."

"Oh, well, I'll get in somehow."

"Don't you want to stand well as a scholar?" she asked.

"I leave that to the poor fellows that have got to work for a living. I am rich."

"You may lose your money."

"I don't mean to."

"Suppose you do?"

"Then I will go to work."

"I should like to have you graduate well at college and then study law. You might get into Congress," said his mother.

"I guess I'll know enough for that," said Godfrey carelessly. "I want to have a good time."

That was not the worst of it, however. He extorted from his mother a large allowance, which he spent at bars and billiard saloons, and one day he was brought home drunk by a schoolfellow.

"Oh, Godfrey, how can you do so?" exclaimed the selfish woman, for once fairly alarmed on another's account.

"Hush up, old woman!" hiccoughed Godfrey.

Mrs. Preston was mortified to think this should be said to her before Godfrey's schoolmate.

"He does not know what he is saying," she said apologetically.

"Yes, I do," persisted Godfrey. "I'm a -- a gen'leman's son. I don't want you to interfere with a gen'leman's son."

He was put to bed and awoke the next morning with a splitting headache. It was the morning of the day which the doctor and Mr. Graves had chosen to call on Mrs. Preston. She was preparing to go out when a servant came upstairs to announce that two gentlemen were in the parlor and wanted to see her.

"Two gentlemen! What do they look like, Nancy?"

"One of 'em looks like he was from the country, mum."

This referred to Mr. Graves, who did have a rustic look. The doctor would readily have passed for a Bostonian.

"Did they give their names?"

"No, mum."

"I will go down directly. I suppose they won't stay long."

Mrs. Preston sailed into the parlor with the air of a city lady, as she proudly imagined, but stopped short in some surprise when she recognized her visitors. Of course, she did not suspect the nature of their business.

Mrs. Preston whirls around the room, imagining herself as a distinguished lady.

Dr. Townley arose as she entered.

"Good morning, Mrs. Preston," he said. "I hope I find you well?"

"I am quite well," said Mrs. Preston coldly, for she had never liked the doctor. She had an unpleasant feeling that he understood her and was not among her admirers. "Good morning, Mr. Graves. You come to the city occasionally?"

"I don't often get time to come up, but the doctor thought I ought to come."

"Indeed! I am sorry to say that I am just going out."

"I must ask you to defer going till we have communicated our business," said the doctor.

"Business?" repeated Mrs. Preston, seating herself in some surprise.

"Yes -- business of importance. In short, your husband's will has come to light."

"My husband's will!" exclaimed Mrs. Preston. "I thought -- "

She checked herself suddenly. She was about to say, "I thought I had destroyed it," and that would have let the cat out of the bag with a vengeance.

"You thought that he left no will," said the doctor, finishing the sentence for her. "He really left two -- "

"Two!"

"That's it -- he executed two -- exactly alike. One he left in my hands."

"That is a likely story!" said Mrs. Preston excitedly. "If that is the case, why, I ask, have we heard nothing of this before?"

"Because it was contained in an envelope, which I was requested not to open for six months after his decease. The time having expired -- "

"May I ask what are the provisions of this pretended will?" demanded Mrs. Preston, in visible excitement.

"Mrs. Preston," said the doctor with dignity, "you appear to forget that you are addressing a gentleman. I am above fabricating a will, as you seem to insinuate. As to the provisions, it leaves five thousand dollars to the town for the establishment of a public library, and five thousand dollars to Andy Burke, besides the small house in which she used to live to the Widow Burke."

The worst had come. In spite of her criminal act, she must lose the ten thousand dollars, and, worst of all, those whom she hated and despised were to profit by her loss.

"This is simply outrageous, Dr. Townley," she said.

"You are speaking of your husband's will, Mrs. Preston."

"I don't believe he made it."

"There can be no doubt of it. Mr. Graves has examined it, and he and myself are so familiar with the handwriting of your husband that we have no hesitation in pronouncing the will genuine."

"Colonel Preston must have been insane if he really made such a will."

"I was his medical adviser," said Dr. Townley quietly, "and I never detected the least sign of an unsound mind."

"The fact of robbing his wife and child to enrich an Irishwoman and her son is proof enough of his insanity."

"Pardon me, madam, but such bequests are made every day. Outside of their legacies your husband left ample fortune, and there is no danger of your being impoverished."

"Did you bring the will with you?"

"No. I did not feel like incurring the risk."

"I shall contest the will," said Mrs. Preston passionately.

"I would not advise you to. The proof of its genuineness is overwhelming. I suppose you never saw the other will?"

Mrs. Preston, at this unexpected question and in spite of her strong nerves, turned pale and faltered. "Of course not," she said after a slight pause.

"Your husband asserts positively in a note to me that he made one," said the doctor, bending his eyes searchingly upon her, for he suspected the truth: that it was distrust of his wife that led Colonel Preston to take the precaution he had done. "Its disappearance is mysterious."

"What do you mean?" cried Mrs. Preston sharply and not altogether without alarm.

"I meant only to express my surprise."

"If your business is over, I will go out."

"I have only this to say that, being named in the will as executor, I shall take immediate measures to have the will admitted to probate. Should you make up your mind to contest it, you can give me due notice through your legal adviser. In that case," he added significantly, "the question of the disappearance of the other will shall come up."

"I will consult my lawyer," said Mrs. Preston.

Though she said this, her determination was already made. "Conscience makes cowards of us all," and the doctor's last hint alarmed her so much that she decided to make no opposition to the execution of the will. But it was a bitter pill to swallow.

"Graves," said Dr. Townley as he left the house, "that woman destroyed the other will."

"Do you think so?" asked Mr. Graves startled.

"I feel sure of it. Let me predict also that she will not contest this will. She is afraid to."

And the doctor was right.

CHAPTER XXXVI

ALL'S WELL THAT ENDS WELL

Andy was quite unconscious of the good fortune which had come to him. Though a manly and stout-hearted boy, he was, in fact, getting discouraged. He was willing and anxious to work, but there seemed to be no work for him to do. He would have left home some time ago to try his fortune elsewhere, but there were the entreaties of his mother, who didn't like to lose him.

In the morning after Dr. Townley's visit to Boston, our hero knocked at the doctor's front door.

"Is Dr. Townley at home?" he asked.

"Yes, Andy," said the doctor, who overheard the inquiry. "Come right in. You're just the boy I want to see."

Andy entered, twirling his hat awkwardly in his hand.

"Good morning, Andy," said the doctor cordially. "Take a seat."

"Thank you, sir," said Andy, but he did not sit down.

"What is the matter? You are looking rather blue this morning."

"Shure, doctor, and that's the way I feel entirely."

"You're not sick, are you? Let me feel your pulse."

"No, I'm not sick, but it's discouraged I am."

"Why should a stout boy in good health be discouraged?"

"I can't get any work to do, and I'm afraid we'll all starve."

"It strikes me," said the doctor, fixing his eyes on Andy and enjoying the effect of his intended announcement, "that I wouldn't talk of starving, if I were as rich as you are, Andy."

"As rich as me?" echoed Andy. "Shure, doctor, you're jokin'."

"Not at all."

"Why, I haven't got but seventy-five cents in the world."

"Now it's you who are joking, Andy."

"I wish I was," sighed Andy.

"Why, I had it on good authority that you were worth five thousand dollars."

Andy stared in earnest.

"I see you're laughin' at me, doctor," he said, suspecting that Dr. Townley was making game of him.

"No, I am not. I am in earnest."

"Who told you such a big falsehood as that, now?" asked our hero, bewildered.

"Perhaps I dreamed that somebody told me Colonel Preston had left you five thousand dollars in his will."

"Are you jokin'? Is it true?" asked Andy eagerly, something in the doctor's face telling him that he really meant what he said.

"Maybe I dreamed, too, that the colonel left your mother the house she used to live in."

"Is it true, doctor? Tell me, quick!" said Andy trembling with excitement.

"Yes, my boy, it's all true, and I'm glad to be the first to congratulate you on your good fortune."

He held out his hand, which our hero seized, and then, unable to repress his exultation, threw up his cap to the ceiling and indulged in an extempore dance, the doctor meanwhile looking on with benevolent gratification.

"Excuse me, doctor; I couldn't help it," he panted.

"It's all right, Andy. Are you discouraged now?"

"Divil a bit, doctor. It's wild I am with joy."

"And you don't think of starving yet, eh, Andy?"

"I'll wait a bit. But why didn't I know before?"

"Sit down, and I'll tell you all about it."

So Andy heard the account, which need not be repeated.

"Now," continued the doctor, "I'll tell you what plan I have for you. Mr. Graves wants to take a boy into his store who will buy an interest in the business and become his partner. He thinks well of you and is willing to take you. What do you say?"

"I'll do whatever you think best, doctor."

"Then I think this is a good opening for you. Mr. Graves wants to retire from business before long. Probably by the time you are twenty-one he will leave everything in your hands. You will be paid weekly wages and perhaps be entitled to a portion of the profits -- more than enough to support you all comfortably. What do you say? Shall we have a new firm in the village? Graves & Burke?"

Andy's eyes sparkled with proud anticipation. It was so far above any dream he had ever formed.

"It's what I'd like above all things," he said. "Oh, what will mother say? I must go and tell her."

"Go, by all means, Andy, and when you have told her, come back, and I'll go over with you to Mr. Graves' store, and we'll talk over the arrangements with him."

Mrs. Burke's delight at her own success and that of Andy may be imagined. She, too, had been getting despondent, and it seemed almost like a fairy tale to find herself the owner of a house and her boy likely to be taken into partnership with the principal trader in the village. She invoked blessings on the memory of Colonel Preston, through whose large-hearted generosity this had come to pass, but she could not help speculating on what Mrs. Preston would say. She understood very well that she would be very angry.

Mrs. Preston did not dispute the will. She might have done so, but for her fear that her own criminal act would be brought to light. Godfrey, who was even more disturbed than she was at the success of "that low Irish boy," begged her to do it, but in this case she did not yield to his entreaties. She had never dared to take him into confidence respecting her destruction of the other will.

While we are upon this subject, we may as well trace out the future career of Mrs. Preston. Some years later she was induced, by the expectation of aiding her social standing, to marry a man who appeared to be doing a flourishing business as a State Street broker. By spurious representations, he managed to get hold of her property and to be appointed Godfrey's guardian. The result may be foreseen. He managed to spend or waste the whole and when Godfrey was twenty-one, he and his mother were penniless. Andy, who was now sole representative of the firm of Graves & Burke, and who was in receipt of an excellent income, heard of the misfortunes of his old enemy, and out of regard to the memory of his old benefactor voluntarily offered Mrs. Preston an allowance of five hundred dollars. It cost her pride a great deal to accept this favor from the boy she had looked down upon as "only an Irish boy," but her necessity was greater than her pride, and she saw no other way of escaping the poorhouse. So she ungraciously accepted. But Andy did not care for thanks. He felt that he was doing his duty, and he asked no other reward than that consciousness. Mrs. Preston was allowed to make her home, rent free, in Mrs. Burke's old house, Andy having built a better and more commodious one, in which he had installed his mother as mistress.

Andy built a beautiful country house for his mother

Mrs. Preston grew old in appearance fast, and she fretted without ceasing for the fortune and position which she had lost. Her second husband left her and has not since been heard of. As for Godfrey, Andy secured him a passage to California, where he led a disreputable life. There is a rumor that he was killed in a drunken brawl in Sacramento not long ago, but I have not been able to learn whether this is true or not. His loss of fortune had something to do with him taking a turn for the worse, but I am afraid, with his character and tendencies, that neither in prosperity nor in adversity would he have built up a good character or led an honorable career. His course had been, in all respects, far different from that of our hero, who, already prosperous, seems likely to go on adding to his wealth and growing in the esteem of the best portion of the community. His success, aided, indeed, by good fortune, has served to demonstrate the favorable effects of honesty, industry, and good principles upon individual success. He is not the first, nor will he be the last, to achieve prosperity and the respect of the community, though he began life as "only an Irish boy."

THE END

~ ~ ~

COMMENTARY FOR
ONLY AN IRISH BOY

By Rick Newcombe

When you read "Only an Irish Boy," you can see clearly that the critics who characterized Horatio Alger's message as "rags to riches" only got it half-right. Yes, the hero of the story, Andy Burke, did indeed rise from being a poor boy in rags to becoming a prosperous storeowner with "an excellent income."

But it is interesting that money is both a blessing and a curse in the world of Horatio Alger Jr. For Mrs. Preston and her son, Godfrey, it is a curse. They are cruel, miserly and arrogant. They are unfeeling and think themselves superior to everyone else in town.

They even go so far as to assert that if Godfrey picks a fight with Andy, and insults Andy's mother, saying, "I don't associate with low people," Andy is supposed to stand by passively and take it. Of course, being Irish, with plenty of spirit, Andy demands that he take it back. Instead, Godfrey throws the first punch, but thankfully it is blocked by Andy, who proceeds to thrash Godfrey.

Colonel Preston, the source of Mrs. Preston's and her son's wealth, is a sensible man throughout the book. So the issue of money with Horatio Alger is not black-and-white. In good hands, wealth is a blessing; in evil hands, it is a curse.

The obsession with money is a reflection of the times. Alger wrote his stories between the years 1865 and roughly 1900. These years began with America struggling financially and in debt immediately after the Civil War. Yet they led to a sustained economic boom -- a growth spurt so substantial that it laid the foundation for the United States to be on its way to becoming the economic envy of the world.

Andy Grant was lucky, yes, but he also made his own luck. He refused to work for a farmer who wanted to exploit him, but when he found the two old maids, Misses Priscilla and Sophia Grant (no relation to then-President Ulysses S. Grant), he worked as hard as he could and did a better job than the man -- yes, full grown man -- who had the job before him. He sensed a kindness and fairness in these two spinsters, and, while still a boy, he was proud to be the "man of the house" by providing them protection and labor.

At the same time, the two sisters were wise enough to realize that Andy needed more education, so they allowed him to go to school in the mornings. He loved it, studied hard and succeeded. He also defended a younger boy against Godfrey's bullying.

Andy had a strong sense of right and wrong, and he was always courageous in defending the good. That was why he did not flinch for an instant when a highway robber held a gun to Colonel Preston.

Andy's mother exuded kindness as well by being the ideal nurse for Colonel Preston when he had a serious illness and almost died. His own wife had abandoned him on the pretext that she was doing it to protect their son.

While a country boy, Andy was very ingenious and quick-witted. Don't forget, he outsmarted a professional con man in Boston -- the very same highway robber who attacked Colonel Preston.

After the sisters announced that they had to move, and thus Andy would lose his job, his world once again looked pretty bleak. But he kept his poise and determined to be on the lookout for new opportunities. When Godfrey confronted him and tried to rub salt in the wound of Andy losing his job, Andy stays calm. They have a sharp exchange of words, and "Godfrey walked away. Somehow, he never could get the better of Andy."

As readers, we see the Will that Colonel Preston left, and we see the evil Mrs. Preston destroying it so she could keep everything. We feel for Andy and his mother. We grow to seethe at the cruelty and piggishness of Mrs. Preston and Godfrey.

Yet Horatio Alger believes this is a just universe, where good is rewarded and evil punished. As it turns out, Colonel Preston suspected his wife might pull a fast one, so he made a copy of the Will and gave it to the town's doctor with instructions to open it six months after his death.

Of course, the result of this was that Andy was given $5,000, which enabled him to buy a partnership in the firm that became GRAVES & BURKE. (In today's dollars, $5,000 would be worth more than $100,000. To find current value for money, Google the words "inflation calculator.")

Mrs. Burke prospered too, first by inheriting the house she had been living in, and then by moving into a much nicer home that Andy built for her.

After Mrs. Preston lost her inheritance by marrying a like-minded swindler, Andy paid her a retainer for life. She was not a bit grateful, but Andy didn't care. "He felt that he was doing his duty, and he asked no other reward than that consciousness."

Isn't his discipline refreshing in this day and age? It is inspiring and one of the keys to success and happiness -- simply to do your duty. In this case, Andy knew this was something his benefactor, Colonel Preston, would have wanted.

At the time this novel was written, the Irish suffered tremendous discrimination in America. Frequently, "Help Wanted" ads included the words, "No Irish Need Apply." It was important to Horatio Alger to defend the downtrodden. We see this as a theme in all of his texts. Andy Burke is called a hero. He is cheerful, optimistic, hard working and kind -- almost to a fault. Yet these are the character traits that enabled him to succeed.

The title for the final chapter of this heartwarming story is, "All's Well that Ends Well," which is life as it should be in Horatio Alger's world. That is one of the main reasons he was such an inspiration to tens of millions of boys for more than a century. We all love happy endings, and Horatio Alger believed they can be as realistic in the real world as they are in his stories.

Rick Newcombe is the founder and CEO of Creators Syndicate, Creators Publishing and Sumner Books.

TEACHERS GUIDE QUESTIONS FOR ONLY AN IRISH BOY

1. The reader is first introduced to Andy Burke when he meets Godfrey Preston. What does Colonel Preston think of his son's demeanor during this encounter? What are Colonel Preston's reasons for defending Andy after the fight?

2. Why does Mrs. Burke stick up for Andy when confronted by Mrs. Preston in Chapter IV? What does this tell you about her character?

3. Andy tells a lie to the Misses Grants. How does he feel about telling such a lie? Does he think of this lie ever again? If so, when and why?

4. What are Godfrey's motives for telling the teacher that Andy attacked him in Chapter XVIII? How does Andy respond?

5. What are some of Andy's best qualities? How does he show these qualities when he sticks up for Alfred Parker in Chapter XVII? What conclusions can you draw about Andy's character?

6. What does Andy do to help Colonel Preston during the colonel's ride back to village? What is your opinion of the way in which Andy behaves towards Mr. Fairfax?

7. Describe the relationship between Andy and his mother. Give at least three examples to support your description.

8. Chapter XXI is titled "A Model Wife." What does this title refer to? Describe the meaning of this title in relation to the events in the chapter.

9. Other than Fairfax's disguise, why does Andy not recognize Fairfax in Chapters 15-18?

10. What prompts Mrs. Preston to discard Colonel Preston's will? How does this bode for her in the subsequent chapters? How does her son's respect towards her change?

TEACHERS GUIDE ANSWERS FOR ONLY AN IRISH BOY

1. Colonel Preston, a fair and just man, thinks his son Godfrey to be ungentlemanly and rightfully worries that he takes after his vain, haughty and proud mother. Colonel Preston defends Andy because Andy only defended himself against Godfrey's physical attack and insults toward his mother.

2. Mrs. Burke sticks up for Andy when confronted by Mrs. Preston because she knows that Andy is a good boy and that Godfrey must have struck Andy first. She does not expect Andy to stand still while he is being assaulted.

3. At first, Andy tells the lie but does not think much about it, as Alger explains that Andy is not a perfect boy. In Chapter X, Andy again thinks of his lie when Sophia Grant encourages Andy to "to improve your time in school, as becomes the great-grandson of such a distinguished orator." Andy feels ashamed that he told this lie and deceived the ladies, and though he does not confess, he vows to always be truthful from thereon out.

4. Godfrey wants to get even with Andy for having knocked him down and embarrassed him in front of everyone. Godfrey concludes that if Mr. Stone does not take sides with him, he will have the teacher fired.

5. Andy confirms the charges that Mr. Stone lies against him and calmly explains that his assaults against Godfrey were in defense of Alfred Parker.

6. Andy is witty, quick thinking and stands up for what is right. He is not afraid to defend himself or others if the cause is just. Andy appears to be a fair and dependable young man.

7.

a. Andy knocks the pistol out of Mr. Fairfax's hand and successfully save Colonel Preston from a highway robbery. He stands his grounds and refuses to be swayed or intimidated by Mr. Fairfax.

b. Andy respects his mother. When Godfrey calls the Widow Burke a "low" person, Andy demands that he take back the insult.

c. Andy takes care of his mother. He builds her a house when he has the means.

8.   The Widow Burke tries to care for Andy as best she can with the means she has. Though she is poor, she makes sure that Andy is fed well and kept for.

9.   The title of the chapter is satirical because Mrs. Preston feigns concern over her husband though she is truly concerned with herself. She puts on a show and appears to be distraught over Colonel Preston's sickness, but the doctor guesses at her selfish intentions. Andy does not recognize Mr. Fairfax because he is not expecting to see him.

10. Mrs. Preston discards Colonel Preston's will because her "selfish nature made her grudge any of her husband's estate to others, except, indeed, to Godfrey." She is aggravated that her husband's wealth should be shared, and she persuades herself that it is right to suppress the will. In the subsequent chapters, the second will is found and executed anyway. Godfrey becomes more unruly and disrespectful towards his mother despite her reproaches.

THE LIFE AND THEMES OF HORATIO ALGER, JR.

By Stefan Kanfer

The Merriam-Webster Dictionary devotes one sentence to him: "Of, relating to, or resembling the fiction of Horatio Alger in which success is achieved through self-reliance and hard work."

True as far as it goes, but that sentence reveals nothing about the man or his accomplishment. Then again, other contemporary reference books are just as terse. Not one acknowledges that Alger in his day (circa 1880-1920) was a publishing phenomenon. During those decades, when a sale of 10,000 volumes was deemed a triumph, readers bought more than 200 million copies of Alger's works, placing him in a league with J.K. Rowling and Stephen King.

Alas, today most of his novels—and there are more than 100— are out of print. But not for long. Thanks to the resuscitation efforts of Sumner Books, a division of Creators Syndicate, Alger's best literary productions are being furnished with fresh covers, new fonts and energetic promotion.

Seldom has there been a more relevant illustration of the maxim that what goes around comes around. At the turn of the 19th century, Alger was the standard-bearer of a phenomenally successful experiment in social reform and personal improvement. That movement inspired disadvantaged kids to move on up, leading juvenile delinquents into productive, significant lives. Men as different as Groucho Marx and Ernest Hemingway were fans.

"Horatio Alger's books conveyed a powerful message to me," wrote Marx, "and to many of my young friends as well—that if you worked hard at your trade, the big chance would eventually come. As a child I didn't regard it as a myth, and as an old man I think of it as the story of my life."

Hemingway's sister Marcelline recalled that during their childhood, "There was one summer when Ernest couldn't get enough of Horatio Alger." Not that Alger's boys' books influenced Papa's prose style. But there must have been something in the writer's stress on grit and self-reliance that affected young Ernest, as it did so many of his contemporaries.

By the end of the Roaring Twenties, though, Horatio Alger had become as passé as the Ford Model T. During the Depression he fared no better; Nathaniel West's satirical 1934 novel, A Cool Million, sent Alger's plots in reverse, as the naïve protagonist loses limb after limb seeking success among rapacious capitalists. Decades later, the film adaptation of Hunter Thompson's 1971 novel, Fear and Loathing in Las Vegas, presented the antihero as "Horatio Alger gone mad on drugs in Las Vegas."

What lay behind Alger's ability to enchant so many Americans—and to enrage so many others? The author's story furnishes a trove of clues:

The sickly child of a Unitarian minister in Marlborough, Massachusetts, Horatio, born in 1832, was always the smallest in his class and far from an academic star. Still, his report cards were good enough for admission to Harvard. There his academic prowess was in inverse proportion to his size (5 feet 2 inches). He won prizes, published verse and fiction in undergraduate magazines, and labeled the entire four years a period of "unmixed happiness."

Decades would pass before he found such contentment again. Upon graduation, Horatio attempted to make his way as a writer. After five unsuccessful years, he returned to Harvard, this time to study at the Divinity School. In 1860 the Reverend Horatio Alger was named minister of the First Parish Unitarian Church of Brewster on Cape Cod. Salary: $800 per year. To supplement his meager income, he turned once again to writing. This time, his stories were well-received, and he allowed himself to dream of a dual career of preacher and writer. That's when catastrophe struck.

It was of his own making, if one historian is to be believed. According to this claim, a 13-year-old told his parents that the new parson had made advances to him. An investigation began. Another lad made a similar complaint. Faced with charges of behaving inappropriately, the accused was allowed to resign—with the proviso that he leave town at once.

Sometime later, Horatio wrote a poem about one Friar Anselmo, who had committed an unspecified crime. Melancholy and remorseful, he comes across a wounded traveler and gives him aid. Whereupon an angel materializes and offers salvation:

Thy guilty stains shall be washed white again
By noble service done thy fellow man.

The fugitive repaired to New York City in the spring of 1866, resolved to live out the Christian ideal, expiating his sin by saving others. The Manhattan he entered was the epicenter of the Gilded Age, a magnet for millions of ambitious climbers, drawn by the post-Civil War boom. Out of sight of the glittering prosperity, the mansions and carriages, however, was another New York, a squalid night town that travelers compared to Calcutta, India.

In The Good Old Days, They Were Terrible, historian Otto Bettmann reports that there was scarcely a slum that pedestrians could negotiate "without climbing over a heap of trash or, in rain, wading through a bed of slime." Many streets were so dangerous that policemen hesitated to walk them alone. A Gramercy Park resident noted in his diary, "Most of my friends are investing in revolvers and carry them about at night"—and the Park was one of the city's better neighborhoods.

The New York City street urchin entered the national consciousness in those years. More than 60,000 neglected or abandoned kids ran unsupervised in the street, partly because of the fallout from the tidal waves of immigration from Europe and partly because of families broken by the Civil War.

What was to be done about these juveniles likely to die on the streets or to end up behind bars? The Reverend Charles Loring Brace founded the Children's Aid Society, designed to take homeless or abused kids away from their corrosive environments. At the same time, John Hughes, New York's first Roman Catholic archbishop, set up parochial schools and a residential institution called the Catholic Protectory, which brought up abandoned or orphaned children to be useful members of society.

Horatio Alger joined these efforts at reclamation. He, too, asked himself what could be done about homeless children. Seeking answers, he wandered through the city's worst neighborhoods. He interviewed "street arabs" who spoke of broken homes, violent confrontations with parents, doomed futures. He observed how their cocky attitudes masked a profound despair. He advised them to get real jobs instead of hanging about, squandering whatever came their way from shining shoes or picking pockets. A handful nodded in agreement, expressing the desire to change their lives; most were content to take life as they found it.

Why, he pondered, did individuals subjected to the same conditions turn out so differently? One boy might become a thief, a sociopath, even a killer. His neighbor, perhaps his brother, might aim to be an upright citizen. What was the difference between them?

What saved certain boys, he came to believe, was a quality that gave them the strength to resist sloth and temptation. In a word, character. But was this inborn? In that case determinism won the day, and change was out of the question. Or, given the right opportunity and attitude, could a dispossessed youth win his share of the American dream? The latter, Alger believed—but only if the boy stopped regarding himself as a victim.

As Alger meditated upon the worst crime of the slums—the stealing of childhood from children—an idea came to him. He would be Brother Anselmo redivivus. He had sinned against youths; now he would rescue them—and in the process save himself. As the novelist put it, by depicting the situation of city waifs, he would "excite a deeper and more widespread sympathy in the public mind, as well as exert a salutary influence upon the class of whom he is writing, by setting before them inspiring examples of what energy, ambition, and an honest purpose may achieve."

Ragged Dick became the template of the fiction to follow. Subtitled Street Life in New York with the Boot Blacks, it charted the rise of a 14-year-old boy from poverty to prosperity. Dick Hunter is an adolescent with all odds against him. He has no family, he smokes, drinks alcohol when he can afford it—not very often on the small change he gets from shining gentlemen's shoes—and sleeps on gratings in the winter.

Yet something separates him from his fellow waifs. He refuses to pick pockets like the others, won't mock his elders, and yearns to "grow up 'spectable.'" His bearing and his innate decency attract the attention of upright New Yorkers. One introduces him to his church; another presents Dick with a few dollars.

The earnest youth resolves to become literate to save his money and live a clean life. One day on a walk near South Ferry he sees a toddler fall in the water. Without hesitation, Dick jumps in and saves the drowning child. In gratitude, the father, an affluent businessman, offers the rescuer a job in his office. Gainfully employed, the onetime vagabond Dick Hunter becomes Richard Hunter Esq., and shuts the door forever on the "old vagabond life which he hoped never to resume."

Naïve? Simplistic? To the jaded, the cynical and the ignorant, yes. But not to thousands of children trapped in the real world of poverty and early death. They got the message of Ragged Dick and demanded more Horatio Alger novels with more moral lessons for them to absorb. Those books changed—and in many cases saved—lives a century before Dr. Martin Luther King Jr. stated his belief that what mattered was not the color of one's skin but the content of one's character.

Today, if you listen closely you can hear, amid the jeers, the escalating sound of the last laugh. In 1947, the Horatio Alger Association was founded. It attracts more prominent men and women now than it did then. The group is dedicated to recognizing American leaders who rose, like Alger's young heroes, from humble origins "through honesty, hard work, self-reliance and perseverance." With grants to U.S. high-school students who have "faced and overcome great obstacles in their young lives," the association encourages them to emulate such enterprising and disparate members as Oprah Winfrey and Ray Kroc, Tom Brokaw and Maya Angelou, Stan Musial and Colin Powell.

They can all testify to the truths that lie between the covers of this volume. Turn the first few pages, and you'll understand why so many followed Horatio Alger's breathless, cliff-hanging chapters leading the way from skid row to success. And why so many more are about to read that map in a world where everything has changed—except the basic truths of life.

Stefan Kanfer is an award-winning writer for City Journal and the author of numerous best-selling books.

ABOUT HORATIO ALGER, JR.

Horatio Alger was born in 1832 in Chelsea, Massachusetts. He spent his early years in the small town and under the guidance of the church and his father, the town pastor, before the family moved just west of Boston to the town of Marlborough. As a shy young boy, Alger poured himself into books and soon became a distinguished student. He studied at Harvard and Harvard Divinity School before becoming a minister. He practiced ministry for a few years near Boston and on Cape Cod, but he was distracted by his true passion: writing. He loved to write, and by 1865 Alger had written a handful of stories, including Frank's Campaign and Paul Prescott's Charge. The latter was the first in a series of stories that would eventually lead to his great success. In 1866, Alger moved to New York to write poetry, newspaper stories and magazine articles. However, he was shocked to find so many homeless and forgotten children among the streets, an unfortunate consequence of the Civil War. He made it his duty to aid the condition of these lost children, both through his stories and by his continuous acts of benevolence.

Horatio Alger became a household name shortly after the Civil War when he began publishing stories in the form of serializations. These serializations were featured in magazines such as Student and Schoolmate and were later compiled as books. Alger's books became enormously popular, especially among teenage boys across the country, and they soon reached millions and millions of readers. Alger continued to produce several stories a year, and, in later years, wrote novels in and of themselves instead of novels from magazine serials.

The years immediately following the Civil War were the same years when the United States emerged as one nation on the road to becoming a worldwide empire. The years between 1865 and 1900 were the years of the empire builders, with the rags-to-riches stories of John D. Rockefeller, Andrew Carnegie, Cornelius Vanderbilt and Thomas Edison. They were the years that laid the foundation for Henry Ford and other business titans and for the spectacular growth of the American economy throughout the 20th century and through today. During these years, Alger published well over 100 stories, poems and novels that spoke to the timeless themes and successes of this era.

The theme of Alger's books is consistent: If you work hard, go the extra mile, are faithful and honest, show kindness and generosity, and maintain a cheerful, positive and optimistic attitude, you will succeed in creating financial security and happiness. On the other hand, if you lie, cheat, steal, are lazy or envious, and try to take advantage of other people, you will be doomed to failure and misery. Despite his background as a preacher, Alger does not make these points in a self-righteous or pontificating way. What he does instead -- just like the parables that Jesus told -- is to create stories that illustrate the virtues that lead to success. And the stories that Alger creates are no ordinary stories. Each one is filled with lively plots and twists and turns, ones that are always unexpected and keep the reader wanting to know what's going to happen next.

As Alger grew older, he continuously strived to write the Great American Novel, little realizing that the rags-to-riches stories he created were more influential than any other novelists'. He travelled out west in early 1877 searching for new material and returned near the end of the year, producing similar stories with a new western backdrop. By 1897, Alger was suffering from asthma, bronchitis and slight short-term memory loss. He moved in with his sister in South Natick, Massachusetts where he spent the last two years of his life.

Most people have never heard of Horatio Alger while some are vaguely familiar with the term "rags-to-riches." In the Alger family, it was the norm to burn correspondence and manuscripts, and this, coupled with Alger's shyness, has greatly kept him from history's limelight. Though too often forgotten today, Alger's works and the themes within them still affect the American psyche. Many assert that there is a lagging spirit in present American culture, that these inspiring stories are irrelevant. Young people are bombarded with external stimuli that make it difficult for them to get to know themselves. Wide-eyed innocence and childlike enthusiasm, once revered as admirable qualities, are sources of mockery and disdain, which makes cynicism and pessimism inevitable. Video games, television shows, movies and music are all aimed at titillating and at seeing who can be the most gritty, violent or shocking. More than a few commentators have used the word "degrading" to describe the assault that children encounter today.

This is unfortunate. Young people need heroes and role models today just as much as they did in the 1870s and '80s, when Alger was creating them at a feverish pace from his New York City apartment, writing as many as four books at a time. Publisher A.K. Loring asserted that Alger's books "captured the spirits of reborn America" for "above all you can hear the cry of triumph of the oppressed over the oppressor ... What Alger has done is to portray the soul – the ambitious soul – of the country." Years later, biographer Edwin P. Hoyt concludes that Alger is "a writer whose influence on the American scene has been so profound that it is hard to measure." Indeed, Alger's works made an overwhelming impression on American culture and society that are still alive with us today. It is for this reason that these classics must be brought to a new generation of readers.

OUR COMMITMENT TO
HORATIO ALGER

By Rick Newcombe

Sumner Books is totally committed to reviving interest in Horatio Alger, one of the best-selling authors of all time yet someone who has been all but forgotten today. I'd like to tell you how this project came about.

Probably the best starting point is to tell you a little about myself. I grew up in suburban Chicago, and my parents were religious and fundamentally optimistic in their outlook on life. They encouraged all eight of their children to be positive in our thinking and hope and pray for the best in all situations. In my adolescence, I discovered many of the self-help authors from the 20th century, including Dale Carnegie, Napoleon Hill and Norman Vincent Peale. I remember reading a small magazine in the 1970s, when I was in my 20s, called Success Unlimited and being inspired each month to work hard and stay positive. The publisher of this magazine was W. Clement Stone, who started his career selling insurance policies door to door and who went on to build Combined Insurance, which became part of Aon, one of the largest insurance companies in the world.

By the time Mr. Stone died in 2002, he was a very successful businessman, an extremely generous philanthropist and totally committed to spreading the gospel of positive thinking. I remember reading one of his books, The Success System That Never Fails, which was both an autobiography and a blueprint for achieving success. Stone told the story of spending a summer on a farm in Michigan when he was 12, getting fresh air, helping on the farm and enjoying picnics, carnivals and camping out.

W. Clement Stone

"But I'll never forget the first day I went upstairs to the attic," he wrote, "for there I met Horatio Alger. At least 50 of his books, dusty and weather-worn, were piled in the corner. I took one down to the hammock in the front yard and started to read."

Stone said he was so enthralled he couldn't stop. "I read through all of them that summer," he wrote.

He said the principle in each book was that "the hero became a success because he was a man of character -- the villain a failure because he deceived and embezzled. How many Alger books were sold? No one knows. Estimates range from 100 million to 300 million. We do know that his books inspired thousands of American boys from poor families to strive to do the right thing because it was right and to acquire wealth."

That was the first time I had heard of Horatio Alger, but it never occurred to me to try to find his books. Over the years, I founded Creators Syndicate, which became one of the most successful newspaper syndication companies in the world. I attribute much of our success to our positive thinking and upbeat attitude. We became a multimillion-dollar international corporation by syndicating a wide variety of journalists, celebrities and award-winning cartoonists.

As we were expanding into new businesses, e-books and audiobooks were a natural starting point because we work with so many talented writers and artists. But we also wanted to try new things. With that in mind, I remembered Mr. Stone's enthusiastic recommendation of Horatio Alger's books, and I decided to read some. Many were available as e-books, and I thoroughly enjoyed them.

I had a good feeling whenever I was transported back to New York City as it was in 1870, when trains were called "cars" and there were no automobiles. There was a constant risk of crossing the streets without streetlights or walk signs. A number of years later, the Brooklyn Dodgers, now the Los Angeles Dodgers, got their name from the treacherous dodging of horses, wagons and streetcars that was required to cross the street in the city. In those days, plumbing with hot and cold running water was not taken for granted, much less radios, televisions, computers or smartphones. Are you kidding? A smartphone in the 1860s? There wasn't even a telephone.

But what great stories Alger wrote -- one after another. I couldn't get enough of them! And it was impossible not to feel grateful for all the modern conveniences of the 21st century when immersing myself in the world of America as it was in the 1860s and '70s.

As I read book after book, I felt like a teenager all over again, excited about the future and the promise of a brighter tomorrow. It was then that I decided to go full bore into spreading the word of Horatio Alger.

One of the problems with the e-books was the lack of organization; another was the maddening number of typos, over and over and over, or the lack of illustrations or the lack of a table of contents. In fact, what was intended to be a good deed to spread Mr. Alger's message really turned out to be something of a disservice.

So I made it my mission to have professional editors edit the texts so there were no typographical or spelling errors. We found appropriate illustrations. We included detailed tables of contents for each book, and we decided to publish them in groups, when appropriate, which has never been done before. We are including commentaries and teachers guides with each e-book.

We also decided to make audiobooks of as many of these "Stories of Success" as possible. We hired a terrific actor, Ben Gillman, and his initial experience shows you how far we have to go to spread the word. Ben went to the Hollywood public library to find some Horatio Alger books, but there was none. "You'd have to go to the downtown public library, in the historical section, to find those," the librarian told him.

Remember, this is one of the best-selling American authors of all time, yet it is as if he never existed.

Part of the problem is that some of the caricatures of Horatio Alger over the years have been absolutely brutal. Even to this day, the Encyclopedia Britannica, from which we expect objective reporting, calls Alger's dialogue and plots "outrageously bad." Come again? The encyclopedia is supposed to provide broad knowledge on specific subjects, not offer the biased literary criticism of a handful of editors. Talk about being unfair -- and just plain wrong!

How do you answer a cheap shot like that? Really, it is nothing more than an incredibly snooty opinion; in fact, it is an "outrageously bad" opinion. Remember, the Horatio Alger books were intended to be not great literature but rather inspirational stories to motivate young boys to achieve a better life. If the dialogue and plots were not lively and believable, the books would not have sold in the millions. The fact that Horatio Alger helped form the American character shows that an incredible number of boys ate up his books as thrilling and believable.

The brilliant writer Stefan Kanfer wrote an extensive review of Horatio Alger's works in 2000 for City Journal magazine, a publication of the prestigious Manhattan Institute. He started off believing the critics, but when he actually read some of Horatio Alger's books, he drew a totally different conclusion. "I began reading the novels aloud to my children," he wrote. "We found them well-plotted, entertaining, and instructive, not at all the righteous antiquities that I had been led to believe. Almost every chapter ends with a cliff-hanger, and all of us could hardly wait for the next night to find out what happened. The conclusions never failed to produce an emotional satisfaction and a feeling that what the author was selling -- independence, forbearance, square dealing -- was well worth buying."

We can only speculate about why the critics have been so harsh on Horatio Alger, but no doubt some it stems from their being turned off by precisely the character traits that Mr. Kanfer identifies. Like it or not, there is a mindset that scoffs at individual achievement through hard work, a positive attitude and generosity -- living every day with an "attitude of gratitude," which is the essence of Horatio Alger's message.

W. Clement Stone was routinely mocked for starting the day by saying, "I feel healthy! I feel happy! I feel terrific!" He encouraged his employees to do the same. In fact, he encouraged everyone to demonstrate outward enthusiasm and PMA, which stood for a positive mental attitude. His critics thought he was ridiculous, but Mr. Stone got the last laugh, living to age 100, which he had set as his goal, and accumulating hundreds of millions of dollars.

Roswell Crawford is an important character in Ragged Dick and Fame and Fortune because he oozes the world-owes-me-a-living attitude that is so common today. "Roswell was troubled with a large share of pride," Alger writes, "though it might have troubled himself to explain what he had to be proud of."

Roswell never understands the importance of integrity and its relationship to earning one's living. In fact, he once says that he would be happy to be paid $10 a week for nothing. "Well, if I get it, I don't care if I don't earn it," he says. In fact, Roswell is ashamed to be seen in the streets carrying a large bundle as part of a delivery for his job. Before being fired, his boss tells him, "You appear to think yourself of too great consequence to discharge properly the duties of your position."

Contrast that with Richard Hunter's attitude toward his entry-level job when he first starts working at the firm. "I'm ready to do anything that is required of me. I want to make myself useful," he says.

I have the impression that was the same attitude that Horatio Alger had as he approached his goal of becoming a successful writer who could change the world -- or at least the world of the thousands of homeless street urchins in the big city. It is difficult to imagine how bad their plight was. For instance, in 1874, which was seven years after Ragged Dick was first published, there was a little girl named Mary Ellen Wilson, who was beaten unmercifully by her stepmother. She was sent out into the streets ill-clothed in winter. There were other abuses, and they were horrible.

So a social worker named Etta Angel Wheeler wanted to intervene, to help get the child out of that environment. But there were no laws to protect children in such situations. Etta was desperate -- and clever. She enlisted the help of the American Society for the Prevention of Cruelty to Animals because animals were protected by law. Her attorneys argued that Mary Ellen, "as a member of the animal kingdom, deserved the same protection as abused animals." This led to new legislation and various child protective services.

Horatio Alger was at the forefront of this movement. He wanted to help the poor kids in the inner city, and he wound up not only helping them but inspiring millions of other young readers across the country. Many of them transformed their lives as a direct result of the inspiration of the "Stories of Success" that Horatio Alger managed to tell in one exciting setting after another.

It is not surprising that Ernest Hemingway's sister said that her brother could not get enough of Horatio Alger or that Walter Brennan, a famous actor for much of the 20th century, devoured his books. As the legendary Groucho Marx said: "Horatio Alger's books conveyed a powerful message to me and to many of my young friends -- that if you worked hard at your trade, the big chance would eventually come. As a child, I didn't regard it as a myth, and as an old man, I think of it as the story of my life."

Groucho was speaking for millions of Americans in the past and, we hope, millions more in the future.

Rick Newcombe is the founder and CEO of Creators Syndicate, Creators Publishing and Sumner Books.

PREVIEW OF ANOTHER ADVENTURE IN THE HORATIO ALGER "STORIES OF SUCCESS" SERIES

ANDY GRANT'S PLUCK

By Horatio Alger, Jr.

If you enjoyed this book, watch for more from the "Stories of Success" series…

"A telegram for you, Andy!" said Arthur Bacon as he entered the room of Andy Grant in Penhurst Academy.

"A telegram!" repeated Andy in vague alarm, for the word suggested something urgent -- probably bad news of some kind.

He tore open the envelope and read the few words of the message:

Come home at once. Something has happened.

MOTHER.

"What can it be?" thought Andy perplexed. "At any rate, mother is well, for she sent the telegram."

"What is it?" asked Arthur.

"I don't know. You can read the telegram for yourself."

"Must you go home?" asked Arthur in a tone of regret.

"Yes. When is there a train?"

"At three this afternoon."

"I will take it. I must go and see Dr. Crabb."

"But won't you come back again?"

"I don't know. I am all in the dark. I think something must have happened to my father."

Dr. Crabb was at his desk in his library -- it was Saturday afternoon, and school was not in session -- when Andy knocked at the door.

"Come in!" said the doctor in a deep voice.

Andy opened the door and entered. Dr. Crabb smiled, for Andy was his favorite pupil.

"Come in, Grant!" he said. "What can I do for you?"

"Give me permission to go home. I have just had a telegram. I will show it to you."

The doctor was a man of fifty-five, with a high forehead and an intellectual face. He wore glasses and had done so for ten years. They gave him the appearance of a learned scholar, as he was.

"Dear me!" he said. "How unfortunate! Only two weeks to the end of the term, and you are our primus!"

"I am very sorry, sir, but perhaps I may be able to come back."

"Do so, by all means, if you can. There is hardly a pupil I could not better spare."

"Thank you, sir," said Andy gratefully. "There is a train at three o'clock. I would like to take it."

"By all means. And let me hear from you, even if you can't come back."

"I will certainly write, doctor. Thank you for all your kindness."

Penhurst Academy was an endowed school. On account of the endowments, the annual rate to boarding scholars was very reasonable -- only three hundred dollars, including everything.

The academy had a fine reputation, which it owed in large part to the high character and gifts of Dr. Crabb, who had been the principal for twenty-five years. He had connected himself with the school soon after he left Dartmouth and had been identified with it for the greater part of his active life.

Andy had been a pupil for over two years and was an excellent Latin and Greek scholar. In a few months he would be ready for college.

Dr. Crabb was anxious to have him go to Dartmouth, his own alma mater, being convinced that he would do him credit and make a brilliant record for scholarship. Indeed, it was settled that he would go, his parents being ready to be guided by the doctor's advice.

From Penhurst to Arden, where Andy's parents lived, was fifty miles. Starting at three o'clock, the train reached Arden station at five.

As Andy stepped on the platform he saw Roland Hunter, the son of a neighbor.

"How are you, Andy?" said Roland with a cheerful greeting. "How do you happen to be coming home? Is it vacation?"

"No. I was summoned home by a telegram. Is -- are they all well at home?"

"Yes, so far as I know."

Andy breathed a sigh of relief.

"I am glad of that," he said. "I was afraid someone in the family might be sick."

"I don't think so. I would have heard, living so near."

"Father is well, then?"

"Come to think of it, I heard he had a bad headache."

"At any rate, it isn't anything serious. Are you going home? If you are, I'll walk along with you."

"We can do better than that. I've got uncle's buggy on the other side of the depot. I'll take you, bag and baggage."

"Thank you, Roland. My bag is rather heavy, and as it is a mile to the house, I shall be glad to accept your offer."

"Bundle in, then," said Roland merrily. "I don't know but I ought to charge you a quarter. That's the regular fare by stage."

"All right! Charge it if you like," rejoined Andy smiling. "Are your folks all well?"

"Oh, yes, especially Lily. You and she are great friends, I believe."

"Oh, yes," answered Andy with a smile.

"She thinks a good deal more of you than she does of me."

"Girls don't generally appreciate their brothers, I believe. If I had a sister, I presume she would like you better than me."

Roland dropped Andy at his father's gate.

It may be said here that Mr. Grant owned a farm of fifty acres that yielded him a comfortable living when supplemented by the interest on three thousand dollars invested in government bonds. On the farm was a house of moderate size which had always been a pleasant home to Andy and his little brother Robert, generally called Robbie.

Andy opened the gate and walked up to the front door, valise in hand.

The house and everything about it seemed just as it did when he left at the beginning of the school term. But Andy looked at them with different eyes.

Then he had been in good spirits, eager to return to his school work. Now something had happened, but he did not yet know what.

Mrs. Grant was in the back part of the house, and Andy was in the sitting room before she was fully aware of his presence. Then she came in from the kitchen, where she was preparing supper.

Her face seemed careworn, but there was a smile upon it as she greeted her son.

"Then you got my telegram?" she said. "I didn't think you would be here so soon."

"I started at once, mother, for I felt anxious. What has happened? Are you all well?"

"Yes, thank God, we are in fair health, but we have met with misfortune."

"What is it?"

"Nathan Lawrence, cashier of the bank in Benton, has disappeared with twenty thousand dollars of the bank's money."

"What has that to do with father? He hasn't much money in that bank."

"Your father is on Mr. Lawrence's bond to the amount of six thousand dollars."

"I see," answered Andy gravely. "How much will he lose?"

"The whole of it."

This, then, was what had happened. To a man in moderate circumstances, it was a heavy blow.

"I suppose it will make a great difference?" said Andy inquiringly.

"You can judge. Your father's property consists of this farm and three thousand dollars in government bonds. It will be necessary to sacrifice the bonds and place a mortgage of three thousand dollars on the farm."

"How much is the farm worth?"

"Not over six thousand dollars."

"Then father's property is nearly all swept away."

"Yes," said his mother sadly. "Hereafter he will receive no help from outside interest and will, besides, have to pay interest on a mortgage of three thousand dollars, at six per cent."

"One hundred and eighty dollars."

"Yes."

"Altogether, then, it will diminish our income by rather more than three hundred dollars."

"Yes, Andy."

"That is about what my education has been costing father," said Andy in a low voice.

He began to see how this misfortune was going to affect him.

"I am afraid," faltered Mrs. Grant, "that you will have to leave school."

"Of course I must," said Andy, speaking with a cheerfulness which he did not feel. "And in place of going to college I must see how I can help father bear this burden."

"It will be very hard upon you, Andy," said his mother in a tone of sympathy.

"I shall be sorry, of course, mother, but there are plenty of boys who don't go to college. I shall be no worse off than they."

"I am glad you bear the disappointment so well, Andy. It is of you your father and I have thought chiefly since the blow fell upon us."

"Who will advance father the money on mortgage, mother?"

"Squire Carter has expressed a willingness to do so. He will be here this evening to talk it over."

"I am sorry for that, mother. He is a hard man. If there is a chance to take advantage of father, he won't hesitate to do it."

BE SURE TO LISTEN TO THE AUDIOBOOK "STORIES OF SUCCESS" SERIES BY HORATIO ALGER, AVAILABLE ON AUDIBLE.COM AND ITUNES. GO TO WWW.SUMNERBOOKS.COM.